**JUSTICE
LOOKS
LIKE...**

JUSTICE LOOKS LIKE...

Reflections on Living the Gospel
in an Unjust World

Eric Black

Editor

1845BOOKS

© 2023 by 1845 Books, an imprint of Baylor University Press
Waco, Texas 76798

All Rights Reserved. No part of this publication may be reproduced, stored in a retrieval system, or transmitted, in any form or by any means, electronic, mechanical, photocopying, recording, or otherwise, without the prior permission in writing of Baylor University Press.

Funding for this project is courtesy of the *Baptist Standard.*

Book design by Kasey McBeath
Cover design by *the*BookDesigners

The Library of Congress has cataloged this book under ISBN 978-1-4813-1924-9.
Library of Congress Control Number: 2023938801

*This book is dedicated to the justice-seekers
whose courage and determination brought us this far.*

The articles in this volume were written in 2020 and published in 2020 and 2021 in the *Baptist Standard* during a period of significant tension around the issue of justice.

The book in your hand was published in 2023. The work of 2020—inherited from the decades before—is still not finished.

What does justice look like to you? How will you bring about your vision of justice?

CONTENTS

1	Introduction to the "Justice looks like . . . " series Eric Black	1
2	What justice looks like in the Old Testament Timothy Pierce	5
3	What justice looks like in the New Testament Stephen Reid	8
4	Justice is providing excellent education for all Charles Foster Johnson	11
5	Justice looks like fighting for children's best interests Alyssa Ross	14
6	Right now, justice looks like righteous anger in action Froswa' Booker-Drew	17
7	Living God's kingdom justice where you are Tony Miranda	20
8	Justice through the eyes of an Arab Israeli Christian R. E.	23
9	Justice looks like making things right John D. Ogletree Jr.	27
10	Justice for immigrants and refugees seldom seen Marv Knox	30
11	Justice looks like hope, not hopelessness Rev. Nell Green	33
12	Justice looks like the kingdom of God Albert L. Reyes	37

13	Justice is making sure Black lives matter Patricia Wilson	40
14	Justice looks like tearing down the wall between you and Christ Bethany Rivera Molinar	43
15	Three ways justice looks like Jesus Patty Lane	47
16	Justice looks like being willing to be uncomfortable Mariah Humphries	50
17	Justice looks like a divine invitation / La justicia es como una invitación divina Nora O. Lozano	53
18	Justice looks like being free of worry Diego Silva	58
19	Images of justice in an emperor's land Rev. Dr. Joseph C. Parker Jr.	61
20	Justice looks like knowing your neighbor Jorge Zayasbazan	64
21	Justice looks like living in the light of justification Kimlyn J. Bender	67
22	Justice looks like an America that can celebrate its diversity Rev. Dr. Michael Evans Sr.	71
23	Justice requires having eyes that see Suzii Paynter March	74
24	Justice requires a biblical—stable—foundation Ricardo Brambila	77
25	Justice looks like anti-racism Jon Singletary	80
26	Justice looks like a healthy relationship Kirk Stowers	83
27	Justice needs you. I need you. Rev. Dr. Kan'Dace Brock	86

28	Learning justice demands all of me Gaynor Yancey	89
29	Justice is the right key to the right door Rev. Cokiesha Bailey Robinson	93
30	Justice must precede peace, calm, and healing Jeremy K. Everett	96
31	Justice looks like jumping in the water Michael Mills	99
32	Justice looks like "fighting for the good of everyone" Cynthia Aulds	101
33	Justice looks like God's law Randy Dale	104
34	Justice looks like a church playground where all can play Joe Rangel	106
35	Justice looks like shalom for my neighbor Anyra Cano	109
36	Justice looks and sounds like "just us" Latisha Waters Hearne	113
37	For many, justice looks far away Hon. Os Chrisman	117
38	Justice looks like a widow not giving up Myles Werntz	119
39	Justice looks like putting out the fire Roy J. Cotton	121
40	Justice looks like my bookshelves Jean Surratt Humphreys	124
41	I never knew I was Black Levi Bedilu	127
42	Justice looks like a Toni Morrison plot Michelle L. Henry	130

43	Justice is something we learn and practice Wes Keyes	133
44	What justice looks like depends on where you're standing Scott Collins	136
45	Justice looks like stepping in and seeking solutions for others Gus Reyes	139
46	Justice looks like all our responsibility Rev. Debra F. Bell	142
47	Justice looks like awakening Nataly Mora Sorenson	145
48	Justice looks like other Mexicans Jesse Rincones	148
49	Justice looks like God's will on earth as it is in heaven Brenda Kirk	151
50	Justice looks like sweeping up injustice Ferrell Foster	154
51	Justice looks like the church serving in the community Jack Goodyear	157
52	True justice looks like restoration and redemption Kristin Houlé Cuellar	161
53	Justice looks like equity in the administration of justice Michael Bell	164
54	For churches, justice should be in the core values Jimmy Dorrell	167
55	Justice looks like wisdom: Abundance vs. scarcity Garrett Vickrey	171
56	Justice looks like the cross Rolando D. Aguirre	174

Contents — xi

57	What justice looks like for families of suspects and defendants Christine Abel Nix	177
58	Justice looks like what Scripture tells us Stephen Reeves	180
59	Justice looks like Onesimus, the bishop of Ephesus Pastor Samuel James Doyle	184
60	Justice looks like leaning into grief Ali Corona	188
61	Justice for mental illness is personal and systemic Jessie Higgins	191
62	Justice is a constant gut check Felisi Sorgwe	194
63	Justice looks like "teaching, modeling, and equipping" Bobby Hall	197
64	Justice involves addressing systemic racism Barry Creamer	200
65	Justice is reflecting God's love in public policy Bee Moorhead	203
66	Justice looks like the best health care for all women Rev. Mary Whitehurst	206
67	Learning about injustice in home financing Ed Francis	209
68	Justice looks like treating all people as God's children Jonathan Fechner	212
69	Justice goes hand in hand with righteousness Justin Lawrence	215

Index of Subjects   219
Index of Scripture   234

1

Introduction to the "Justice looks like . . . " series

Eric Black

In a long line of unarmed Black men and women killed by police and vigilantes—including Botham Jean in Dallas, Texas (September 6, 2018); Atatiana Jefferson in Fort Worth, Texas (October 12, 2019); Ahmaud Arbery near Brunswick, Georgia (February 23, 2020); and Breonna Taylor in Louisville, Kentucky (March 13, 2020)—George Floyd, killed by former Minneapolis police officer Derek Chauvin May 25, 2020, stands as a breaking point for many of us.

The rapid succession of Arbery's, Taylor's, and Floyd's killings brought our nation and me to a boil. I knew I must do something, and the *Baptist Standard* needed to do something, but what? What could the *Baptist Standard* do to make a difference in favor of justice?

Then it occurred to me. The purpose of the Voices column of the *Baptist Standard* is to let Baptists in Texas speak for themselves. Rather than using my editorials to tell our readers what justice is, I could invite those with more authority on the topic to tell us themselves. In a flash, "Justice looks like . . . " was born.

Justice is universal

Justice is simultaneously universal and personal. Justice is central to God's character and God's interaction with creation. Being stitched into creation, justice will not be ignored or go unmet. Scripture makes that clear numerous times.

As one example, the messianic promise of Isaiah 42 reads, "[My chosen one] will bring justice to the nations . . . In faithfulness he

2 — Introduction to the "Justice looks like..." series

will bring forth justice; he will not falter or be discouraged till he establishes justice on earth" (Isaiah 42:1, 3–4). When creation is unjust, the Creator will make sure justice is accomplished.

As if to prove the point, justice seems to be on everyone's mind and lips these days. Scroll through your social media feed or the headlines, and you will see appeals for justice everywhere.

Protests, economic concerns, health disparities, racial reconciliation, foreign relations, law enforcement, gender, politics, money, power, health care, education, voting—matters of justice are involved in all of these headline makers. Justice—matters of right and wrong and setting things right—is of concern to us all.

Justice is personal

Despite our common concern for justice, universal justice is so difficult for us to achieve in part because we each have a differing view of it. We come to blows over justice because we aren't sure what's right for someone else won't result in what's wrong for us. Even that last sentence can start a fight.

If we are to work toward justice, we must find some common ground. A starting place might be simply to listen to one another—to hear each other out. In "Justice looks like..." we will do just that. We will hear from people not like us. We will listen to people from numerous backgrounds and perspectives.

About the article series

"Justice looks like..." was originally published as a special series in the Voices column of the *Baptist Standard* to provide an opportunity for followers of Jesus to listen to each other. Articles were not grouped by theme at that time, nor are they here. Rather, they were published in a somewhat random order. Articles were mixed as much as possible by author ethnicity and gender to enable each writer's voice and perspective to stand on its own.

The only parameter given to writers was that they provide their perspective on justice from their unique vantage point, understanding that the undergirding intent of the series is to give voice to numerous perspectives on justice, how justice is involved in many—if not all—areas of life, and how Christians can engage one another and our world in enacting God's justice.

Though the Voices column features writers from churches, institutions, and organizations affiliated with the Baptist General Convention of Texas, the "Justice looks like . . . " series included some writers not so directly connected to the BGCT. Of one hundred people invited to participate, sixty-eight responded with the articles republished here in a single volume. I am profoundly grateful for each person who responded and wrote an article. The short bio at the end of each article identifies where the writer was at the time the article was originally published. Any changes are noted.

The series ran from July 29, 2020, to November 22, 2021. One article was published each week to allow readers to give more focused attention to each perspective and to listen to the pain, anger, grief, and hope expressed in each. Though the articles may seem to be a snapshot of American society during the height of the COVID-19 pandemic, their relevance and calls to action are no less significant today.

To ground the series in Christian Scripture, the first article published after the introduction was on justice in the Old Testament, followed the next week by an article on justice in the New Testament. Other articles subsequently published returned to examine justice in the Bible.

One thing "Justice looks like . . . " writers hold in common is Jesus Christ—the physical embodiment of God's perfect justice and the fulfilment of God's law. In seeking to be faithful followers of Jesus Christ, these writers ground their understanding of justice in God's character and word.

A note about style: When initially published, article manuscripts were edited to conform to the *Associated Press Stylebook*. Some changes have been made to conform the articles to the *Chicago Manual of Style* for this publication. Online reading favors shorter paragraphs. Therefore, longer paragraphs were broken, sometimes into single sentences. The shorter paragraph format has been retained here to retain the feel of online journalism.

Justice touches a nerve

Talk of justice often makes us nervous. We feel suspicious, guarded, defensive, or overwhelmed. Indeed, "Justice looks like . . ." challenged readers at times and in ways some didn't want to be challenged. Most received the series well, however, and many expressed their appreciation that it was published.

Hoping to set the tone for "Justice looks like . . .", I ended the original series introduction with the following words from the Apostle Paul about Christians' common bond and what it means for us who follow Jesus:

> Be completely humble and gentle; be patient, bearing with one another in love. Make every effort to keep the unity of the Spirit through the bond of peace. There is one body and one Spirit, just as you were called to one hope when you were called; one Lord, one faith, one baptism; one God and Father of all, who is over all and through all and in all. . . .
>
> So Christ himself gave the apostles, the prophets, the evangelists, the pastors and teachers, to equip his people for works of service, so that the body of Christ may be built up until we all reach unity in the faith and in the knowledge of the Son of God and become mature, attaining to the whole measure of the fullness of Christ. (Ephesians 4:2–6, 11–13)

Dr. Eric Black is the executive director, publisher, and editor of the Baptist Standard.

2

What justice looks like in the Old Testament

Timothy Pierce

When one talks about the language of justice in the Old Testament, there are terms directly translated as *justice* or associated concepts, and there are those that create a platform upon which the concept of justice rests.

Where justice begins

All discussions of justice and how humanity treats humanity begin, continue, and end with the central concept of humanity being created in the "image of God" (*tselem elohim*). The fact that everyone—male and female—is created in the image of God (Genesis 1:27) is the basis for ethics and morality throughout the entirety of Scripture.

Indeed, since this is the essence of how we are created, all standards of treatment are built around either maintaining this status in society or returning individuals to this standing when it has been lost.

From this central premise, the Old Testament branches out in a variety of directions to express more precisely how one might maintain such a status.

Words in the Old Testament

Shaphat and mishpat

The first term for the word *justice* is found in the verb *to govern or judge* (*shaphat*) and its related noun *judgment* (*mishpat*). These terms have their basis in a legal setting.

The meaning, however, does not stop simply at rendering *judgment*, as in a decision or act of applying legal or moral standards to a situation or relationship. It also expresses an attitude, right, or desire for rectitude that belongs inherently to individuals because of their position in society or their identity as an image-bearer (Exodus 23:6; Micah 6:8).

Tsedeq

While one often thinks of the term *righteousness* (*tsedeq*) in terms of expressing a person's standing before God, it is also used for how people treat other people. In fact, there are several places in Scripture where righteousness is put alongside justice almost as a synonym or explanation (Psalm 89:14; Proverbs 21:3).

Tsedeq can carry the idea of vindication or, more generally, the act of setting something right. Since this word plays such a central role in both salvific and social contexts, one can see how closely Scripture connects our relationship with God to our relationship with man.

Indeed, at the heart of the holiness code and covenant stipulations of Leviticus 19 and Deuteronomy 16 is the precept that our righteousness from God must result in justice for people. Prophets such as Amos and Micah make this connection explicit in a couple of places (Amos 5:6–7, 14–15, 24; Micah 6:8).

Din

An often-overlooked term, *din* is almost a synonym of *mishpat* but finds expression almost solely in poetic and worship texts rather than in legal or narrative contexts. It is often communicated in relation to a plea, and in most of its occurrences it refers to defending, protecting, or restoring the oppressed or weak (Jeremiah 5:28, 22:16; Psalm 9:5, Psalm 140:13; Proverbs 31:5, 8; Job 35:14).

Meshar

Equity (*meshar*) literally means that something is level or straight and is used figuratively in wisdom-centered texts to refer to the ethical value of seeking equity or justice (Proverbs 1:3, 2:9, 8:6; Psalm 9:9, 58:2, 75:3; Isaiah 33:15; Daniel 11:6).

Wise living values equity. Many scholars connect the basic Hebrew idea of wisdom (*hokmah*) with the Egyptian concept of harmony (*ma'at*). In Egyptian iconography, a person's soul often was balanced or weighed by the feather, which represented *ma'at*. This connection shows the Hebrew concept of wisdom is yet another way in which we see the call for balance or justice as a fundamental path of life in Scripture.

Other views of justice in the Old Testament

There are many other places one could look to understand better the idea of justice in the Old Testament.

The whole concept of the year of jubilee, during which debts were forgiven and land was returned, was rooted at least in part in maintaining equality, overcoming injustice, communicating righteousness, and emphasizing the link between salvation and justice (Leviticus 25; Isaiah 58:6–12).

Prophets, at times, used the language of sexual perversion to describe the social injustice that took place in Israel (Ezekiel 9:9; Hosea 1–3).

The central story of the entire Old Testament is the Exodus, which begins with four terms expressing God's total identification with the oppressed (Exodus 2:23–25).

Wherever one turns in the Old Testament, it is impossible to separate the concepts of belonging to God and carrying out justice in the world in which we live. It is built into creation itself.

Timothy Pierce is associate professor of Christian studies at East Texas Baptist University.

3

What justice looks like in the New Testament
Stephen Reid

Justice is universal, personal, and contextual all at the same time. By *contextual* here, I mean Baptist. For Baptists to ask what justice looks like requires "looking to Jesus the author and perfecter of our faith" (Hebrews 12:2).

Justice looks like treating every person as you would treat Jesus. It moves beyond cosmetic niceness and providing hospitality for the worthy poor. The King of kings takes the place of the poor and unwanted and frames Christian views of justice.

Jesus' last teaching (Matthew 25:40–46) before the passion story (Matthew 26:1–27:66) defines justice as radical hospitality. It moves beyond a sense of hospitality for the worthy.

The most compelling metric for justice remains how we have treated the least of these (Matthew 25:45). Our position on mass incarceration looks different if we picture Jesus in prison. Our position on immigration looks different if we see Jesus as a migrant. Our position on women looks different if we see Jesus as a woman.

Jesus does not soften the blow for those who miss this metric (Matthew 25:46). Jesus makes clear the Christian community is moving into a time of reckoning (Matthew 25:31–39).

Justice looks like the good Samaritan

I often hear preached the story of the good Samaritan (Matthew 22:34–40; Mark 12:28–31; Luke 10:25–37). It is part of nice people's gospel.

A young lawyer comes to test Jesus with a trick question: "What must I do?" In some ways, the lawyer asks, "What do justice and salvation look like?"

Jesus provides an orthodox response drawn from the Scriptures of the Jewish people: Love God (Deuteronomy 6:5) and neighbor (Leviticus 19:17–18).

The lawyer presses Jesus with the question, "Who is my neighbor?"—a question that challenges Christians still today.

Jesus responds with a story about a survivor of a violent crime. Three characters have the opportunity for justice and love. Only one responds correctly.

The preacher then segues into "Go, and do likewise." By that, the preacher means, "Extend generous hospitality to the survivors of violence." Such a sermon overlooks how Jesus transgresses social norms.

We like to think, "Do what the Samaritan did." Jesus, rather, asks the believer to *be* a Samaritan.

When Jesus, through his work on the cross, becomes despised for our salvation, he defines justice. It is more than generosity; it is an act of relinquishing privilege.

Justice looks like Simon of Cyrene

Justice looks like a character we often ignore. Simon, who carried the cross of Christ, was from Cyrene, in northern Africa, in what today is eastern Libya. He was not a Samaritan, but he carried the cross of Christ (Matthew 27:32).

Simon of Cyrene was played by two well-regarded actors—by Paul Robeson, in the play *Simon the Cyrenian* (1920), and by Sidney Poitier, in the movie *The Greatest Story Ever Told* (1965). The playwright Ridgely Torrence and the filmmaker George Stevens wanted to invite viewers to imagine an African presence in early Christianity. Their selection of Robeson and Poitier, respectively, indicates their attempt to make an African presence in early Christianity more acceptable.

The good Samaritan and Simon of Cyrene both gesture to a justice rooted in the cross of Christ. The theologian James Cone in his book *The Cross and the Lynching Tree* makes clear the connections between the spectacle of lynching in the United States and the crucifixion of Jesus. The cross was the lynching tree of Jesus.

Justice looks like choosing the lynching tree

The thousands of women, children, and men lynched did not choose their fate. The purpose of the spectacle of lynching was to imprint into the imagination of the community the power of the empire in the time of Jesus and the power of white supremacy in the America of the nineteenth and twentieth centuries.

But even in the festival of blood that constitutes a lynching, God can make a testimony of justice on the horizon. When Jesus says to his disciples, "Take up your cross and follow me" (Matthew 16:24), his invitation is to the lynching tree.

Justice looks like treating every person as if that person were Jesus. That kind of radical hospitality likely leads a Christian to a lynching tree. The world thinks justice leads to progress and niceness.

Instead of niceness and progress, Christians and Baptists hope for resurrection and God's redemption of the universe.

Dr. Stephen Reid at the time of writing was professor of Christian Scriptures at Baylor University's Truett Theological Seminary. He is now Vice Provost for Faculty Diversity and Belonging at Baylor University.

4

Justice is providing excellent education for all

Charles Foster Johnson

If Old Testament theologian Walter Brueggemann is correct in defining justice making as figuring out what belongs to whom and giving it to them, then we must support universal education for all children.

Education provides the ability to name God's world. As the first human did at the feet of God in the wonderful creation story recorded in Genesis 2, discovering and naming our world is the enterprise that makes us fully human. In order to "be fruitful, multiply, replenish the earth, and subdue it," we must engage in this labeling and categorizing project.

As any learner and teacher knows, humans do not "have dominion" over any reality until and unless they understand it, label it, and identify it. Such activity constitutes our humanness. It distinguishes us from the rest of the natural order.

Being human is in a name

In Genesis 2, this naming is listed with two other activities. First, the human is placed by God in a garden of provision with that marvelous command, "You may eat."

Then, at the end of the chapter, the human is introduced to another human, at which magical moment he exclaims, "At last, bone of my bone, flesh of my flesh." In an ingenious flourish, God commands the human to "cleave" to the other human, thus establishing the gift of relationship, marriage, family. The gift of love.

Long before Abraham Maslow theorized his famous hierarchy of needs, the word of God outlined a similar dynamic order in explaining human motivation and behavior. First, our physical needs are primal and primary. Second, language and learning—the naming impulse—are necessary for us to advance to a fruitful subduing of the earth. Third, love and the quest for self-awareness and self-identity are the highest, noblest impulses of humans.

Education is essential for both human sustainability and provision, on the one hand, and self-actualization and discovery, on the other. This is why justice—what belongs to whom—looks like quality education for all children everywhere, a provision only secured if accepted as a universal human right and provided as a necessary public trust.

Public education and the social contract

There simply are not enough personal human resources, nor is there enough philanthropic human motivation, for education to be left to private enterprise. If education is to be extended equitably to all children regardless of class, race, gender, and religion, it must be secured and provided by the public.

In our confused season, when the very word "public" suffers much suspicion, what this means is everyone in the community invests in the education of everyone in the community.

Public education is integral to the social contract we make with one another as citizens. If we "hold these truths to be self-evident, that all men are created equal and endowed by their Creator with certain unalienable rights, among them life, liberty, and the pursuit of happiness," then we must—by logical extension of this conviction—provide equal education for all.

When our forebears launched the American experiment 244 years ago, they knew the only hope for sustaining their revolution in human affairs would be for all their fellow citizens to be as educated as they were. Thus, they began a conversation about education provided by public tax dollars.

Some decades later, in the 1840s, that conversation became implemented in policy, first in Massachusetts. By the latter part of the nineteenth century, every state constitution had a statute calling for mandatory education paid for by the public.

Naming the gap

We have a long way to go in making this institution of American life truly just and equitable for all children. Because local tax dollars, chiefly through property taxes, underwrite the costs of public schools, all too often a child's zip code determines the quality of that child's education.

While state and federal law demands equity—namely, that publicly provided education must be uniformly executed regardless of the economic level of the community—we have fallen far short of realizing that lofty goal.

Furthermore, because public education serves the sector of the body politic least likely to advocate for their own interests—children—we have seen that public school funding has not kept pace with our children's educational needs.

Tragically, we now have powerful forces seeking to demonize public schools as "failed" to divert their already depleted funding to underwrite private schools through school vouchers and to privatize them for the financial gain of a few.

These unjust policies subvert the purpose of public education by making it a commodity only for those who can afford it rather than a social good for all.

What does justice look like? Great public schools for all children, the crown jewels of our nation and neighborhoods.

Charles Foster Johnson is founder and executive director of Pastors for Texas Children and pastor of Bread Fellowship in Fort Worth.

5

Justice looks like fighting for children's best interests

Alyssa Ross

I am a public-school teacher, an adoptive mom, and a sister of a woman with Down syndrome. I am a Bible-believing woman with a desire to fight for every person to know Jesus' love and to love him in return.

Special education

Growing up, I watched my parents advocate for my sister's education. Quite literally, they fought for her right to be taught how to read.

The public school system thought Angela needed to be taught social skills, but they didn't believe she could learn to read. My parents believed differently, and Mom would sit in ARD meeting after ARD meeting, advocating for her child's right to be taught *how to read*. (ARD stands for Admission Review and Dismissal, which determines a child's placement in or release from special education.)

As a public-school teacher today with a passion for enabling children to learn and grow in the least restrictive environment, I was blown away by this. Did those teachers forget Angela needed to read a menu, a street sign as she walked home from the park, a label, or price tag on a shirt?

I am not naïve. I know she's not going to read Tolstoy. But reading is a part of living life. Justice for Angela included learning how to read. Angela needed an advocate to fight for her.

Adoption

In high school, I had my first personal look at adoption when my music minister's sister adopted a little girl. I knew I would be a part of that world, someday. At age thirty-two, someday arrived, and I became a licensed foster single parent.

After the privilege of fostering five little girls over seven years, I adopted twelve-year-old Mia. She is now a teenager and a joy of my heart. I would love for her to stay innocent, but I can't allow her to stay innocent and still be prepared for this world.

When Mia first came into my home several years ago, people asked me if she "was an illegal," because of her Hispanic heritage.

She has gorgeous, thick, dark brown hair that will do anything she wants. Her huge smile with white flashing teeth makes me smile because it's bubbling with joy. And I'm not worried about her like I would be if she were Black. But I do know she will encounter racism, and we talk about it regularly. Each time a Black man or woman has been killed, we talk about it again.

It is my job to educate her, to encourage her to stand up for others, to be prepared when someone acts in a threatening way toward her because of her gender or ethnicity or both. I said "when," not "if." But I don't feel like it's enough.

How do I, as a white woman with white privilege and wealth privilege—and that's coming from a single mom who is a teacher—talk with my Hispanic daughter about racism, knowing she will experience it, but not as badly as a Black friend, and that she needs to be able to stand up for herself *and* others? I don't have the answers. All I know is we have to have the conversations.

Justice for Mia includes a loving, safe home and a forever family. Justice for Mia, and all children of minority ethnicities, includes having hard conversations. Our children need an advocate willing to do difficult things.

Public education

I have taught in public schools for eighteen years. There have been times when parents and I worked as a team because they did not know what to do to help their children grasp a difficult academic concept or learn social skills or have strong character qualities.

There are times when I sat in ARDs and handed tissue to parents processing information they knew was coming but was still hard to hear. There are times a test doesn't show what I know a child can do.

Justice for our children means someone is willing to fight for their best interests. Our children need an advocate to fight for them.

In Proverbs 31:8, King Lemuel's mother taught him well: "Open your mouth, judge righteously, and plead the cause of the poor and needy."

We cannot remain silent. We cannot stand by inactively. We must speak up, and we must stand up when someone—anyone—needs us to advocate for them. That is what justice looks like to me.

Alyssa Ross has been a public school teacher and advocate for children from hard places for more than twenty years. She is a member of Citizens Church, previously The Village Church Plano campus.

6

Right now, justice looks like righteous anger in action

Froswa' Booker-Drew

> . . . let justice roll down like waters,
> and righteousness like an ever-flowing stream. (Amos 5:24)

I was on a call recently with a group of women involved in ministry. Some are ministers. Others are teachers. Several are in leadership roles at their churches.

As we discussed our issues serving in the church, one of the ladies asked a question about the challenge of being perceived as angry and the stereotype that accompanies the perception of a woman who speaks up.

I have been wrestling with this idea of anger. As a society, we are more comfortable with rage and other manifestations of anger, like hate, than we are with displays of righteous anger, which Jesus demonstrated.

In the Gospel of Matthew, we see Jesus upset with something he witnessed. He saw the house of God being used for something other than what it was intended for.

"Jesus entered the temple courts and drove out all who were buying and selling there. He overturned the tables of the money changers and the benches of those selling doves. 'It is written,' he said to them, 'My house will be called a house of prayer, but you are making it a den of robbers'" (Matthew 21:12–13).

Jesus exhibited righteous anger. He did not stand back and watch injustice occur. In that moment, he did not just speak up; he did something.

Many would describe his anger as righteous anger. Righteous anger is a response to the mistreatment of others and to sin.

Righteous anger speaks out

In this season, when righteous anger not only is needed but is critical, much of the church has remained quiet, refusing to speak out on behalf of those who are part of the body of Christ.

As we witness racial injustices against Black Americans, there has been a deafening silence from pulpits and congregations across our country.

I am reminded of a parable in Luke 15: "Suppose one of you has a hundred sheep and loses one of them. Doesn't he leave the ninety-nine in the open country and go after the lost sheep until he finds it? And when he finds it, he joyfully puts it on his shoulders and goes home. Then he calls his friends and neighbors together and says, 'Rejoice with me; I have found my lost sheep.' I tell you that in the same way there will be more rejoicing in heaven over one sinner who repents than over ninety-nine righteous persons who do not need to repent" (Luke 15:4–7).

Jesus is not saying the ninety-nine sheep are not important, but when one is lost and needs to be reunited and returned to the flock, it is important that we find that sheep and bring it back into the fold.

Love at the core of God's will

At the core of justice is God's will and an understanding that without love, we are like clanging cymbals (1 Corinthians 13:1). We create noise that continues to divide and separate the church. Our lack of love could be the very thing driving away those to whom we are called to serve and minister.

First John 4:20–21 says, "Whoever claims to love God yet hates a brother or sister is a liar. For whoever does not love their brother and sister, whom they have seen, cannot love God, whom they have not seen. And he has given us this command: Anyone who loves God must also love their brother and sister."

Right now, justice looks like the righteous anger of Jesus.

Right now, justice looks like reconciliation and repentance and restoration.

Right now, justice requires speaking up on behalf of those who have been separated from the body of Christ because of racism and discrimination.

Right now, justice is love for those who do not look like us or live the way we do.

I pray we begin to live and embody the Lord's prayer: "Your kingdom come, your will be done on earth as it is in heaven."

Dr. Froswa' Booker-Drew is a member of the board of directors of Buckner International; the former national director of community engagement for World Vision, US Programs; and the former vice president of community affairs and strategic alliances for the State Fair of Texas. She is a member of Cornerstone Baptist Church in South Dallas under the leadership of Pastor Chris Simmons.

7

Living God's kingdom justice where you are
Tony Miranda

Last summer, I taught the course Ministering in the Latino Context, which covers many aspects of Latino culture and its implications in ministry.

In the class, there were four Black students. I learned from listening to their stories that many of the social and racial injustices Latinos suffer in this country have tenors similar to other minorities' experiences, not only in the African American context but also in all the subcultures of this nation.

Imperfect and perfect justice

Indeed, the drums of social and racial discrimination have been beating louder in the heart of American society in recent days. The truth is we always will be looking to improve our system of justice, and this will be an unending journey.

Recent events that have ignited the social and racial agendas are ample evidence that our concept of social justice is far from perfect. Clearly, it is an incomplete, adulterated, and imperfect human system.

The different manifestations and expressions of unconformity about social racism reveal only the tip of the iceberg, the reality of which communicates a desperate need to get closer to racial reconciliation in different parts of the world.

At the same time, we must never forget all human systems of justice, at their best, still are far from the perfect justice imparted by God in his kingdom.

In the same way human laws are far from perfection, the system that administrates the application of those laws also is imperfect. Thankfully, this is not the case with divine justice since God's law is perfect, and he administers his kingdom in accordance with his justice. Both God's law and justice are perfect.

The biblical call has not changed. "Hacer justicia y amar misericordia"—"Do justice, and love mercy" (Micah 6:8). As Christ's followers, we know seeking first God's kingdom and his justice constitute the foundation of this journey. It is our responsibility to search for his will to be done on earth as it is in heaven since it is only in his will that justice finds its perfect fulfillment.

Three biblical terms for justice

In both the Hebrew and Greek Scriptures, justice is a virtue with particular prominence in the commandment of loving our neighbor (Leviticus 19:18).

Mishpat (מִשְׁפָּט) is a Hebrew term that gives a restorative sense of justice from a legal viewpoint—as used in Micah 6:8, quoted above.

At the same time, *tzedeq* (צֶדֶק)—seen in Deuteronomy 16:20—is a concept of social justice and solidarity with the more vulnerable that gives value to their dignity.

In the New Testament, the Greek term *dikaiosuné* (δικαιοσύνη) is seen as a virtue that belongs to God, and citizens of his kingdom ought to seek it (Matthew 6:33).

These three terms for justice are spread throughout Scripture as essential in the fulfillment of God's will.

Embodying kingdom justice

As Christ's disciples, we need to listen to the words and follow the steps of our Master. Jesus did much to bring down the religious, cultural, economic, racial, and political barriers within and outside his context.

In *Kingdom Ethics*, David Gushee and Glen Stassen rightly assert, "Kingdom is something we do, not just wait for."[1]

---

[1] David Gushee and Glen Stassen, *Kingdom Ethics: Following Jesus in Contemporary Context*, 2nd ed. (Grand Rapids: Eerdmans, 2016), 13.

Kingdom praxis, such as justice, healing, racial reconciliation, community building, and deliverance, are part of this endeavor, which Christians need to present as the biblical response to the different forms of social injustice.

We are not to be conformed to worldly systems but are to be transformed in our minds—and hearts, in the Hebrew context—to "act justly and to love mercy" toward our neighbor in its different biblical expressions—*mishpat, tzedeq,* and *dikaiosuné.*

How many Vanessa Guillens and George Floyds still exist in our world? How many of us are willing to heal those wounds, to bring the presence of Christ among those people?

Living justice where you are

As a Latino, my call is not only addressed toward those discriminated against because of their skin tone or accent and the social injustice Hispanics commonly suffer as immigrants or marginalized people in the barrios—Spanish-speaking neighborhoods.

As a follower of Christ's example, my call is to act opposite of every kind of injustice within and outside my context, starting with my own *oikos*—"family" or "home." Similarly, what can you do in your *oikos* to minimize the social injustice around you?

For now, as we do our best to get closer to the ideal of divine justice, let's claim together, "Que venga pronto tu Reino Señor"—"May your kingdom come soon, Lord" (Matthew 6:10).

Dr. Antonio Josué Miranda is the pastor of Primera Iglesia Bautista in Austin and author of Las Parábolas de Jesús en su Contexto. *He has served as president of the Hispanic Baptist Convention of Texas and has taught for Southwestern Baptist Theological Seminary, Midwestern Baptist Theological Seminary, Seminario Teológico Bautista Mexicano, and other institutions. He and his wife, Daleth, have three beautiful daughters.*

8

Justice through the eyes of an Arab Israeli Christian

R. E.

I am an Arab evangelical Christian. I also am an Israeli citizen by birth. I speak Arabic, Hebrew, and English fluently and was raised in a dual traditional Catholic/Greek Orthodox household.

When I came to Christ in my early twenties, I chose to worship with an evangelical Christian church, further distorting my complicated identity. My passport says, "citizen of Israel"—by definition a Jewish state—but my ancestry is fully Palestinian.

My physical features are undoubtedly Arab. My beard and darker skin are hallmarks of my heritage. Intense airport screenings, public searches, and hours-long questioning are the norm whenever I travel.

I grew up simultaneously accepted and rejected across multiple aspects—accepted as a citizen of Israel, but rejected as equal to a Jewish citizen; accepted as Arab, but rejected as a true Palestinian because I am not Muslim; accepted as Christian by the tiny core of evangelical believers of the Holy Land, but rejected by the Catholic and Orthodox churches because evangelicalism is considered a cult. The list goes on and on.

Justice in the Bible and Jesus

What exactly is justice? The word *justice* is ascribed to the idea of fairness and moral righteousness. It demands both equality and equity and often is associated with the biblical ordinance of an "eye for an eye." In simple terms, it levels the playing field.

The Bible abounds in instruction on the seeking and implementing of justice for all, with special emphasis on the marginalized and oppressed. We are told to "give justice to the weak and the fatherless; maintain the right of the afflicted and the destitute" (Psalm 82:3) and to "learn to do good; seek justice, correct oppression" (Isaiah 1:17), among other things.

For believers, Jesus represents the ultimate expression of justice, with his sacrifice allowing all people access to God the Father.

Segregation in Israel and Palestine

Because I grew up in Israel and the Palestinian territories, my earliest memories center around an unspoken understanding of segregation.

Arab children were not allowed to learn in the same school as Jewish children but nevertheless were required by law to learn to speak Hebrew.

Outrage, frustration, and hopelessness were common emotions as we learned of family members and friends who were forced from their ancestral homes, stripped of jobs, denied exit and entry rights from their own towns, and indiscriminately terrorized and imprisoned.

We practiced "bomb drills" and experienced a war every couple of years.

Everything about our lives as Arabs was separate but certainly not equal. We had our own hospitals, markets, and civic organizations separate from our Jewish neighbors but nevertheless overseen by them and completely at their mercy.

We existed as second-class citizens. On paper, we belonged; in reality, we were shunned at worst and uncomfortably tolerated at best. The divisions flowed down into our towns and villages, with Muslims and traditional Christians living in a tenuous relationship strengthened in collaboration against Jewish persecution and weakened by internal mistrust and suspicion.

Growing up, I had limited interactions with non-Arab children and formed no real relationships with non-Arabs until I reached high school. This is an astounding feat when you consider how densely populated the nation of Israel is, with Arabs and Jews living practically shoulder to shoulder.

Western church blind to Arab Christians

When I became a follower of Christ, I joined a tiny group of believers representing less than 1 percent of the population of Israel. It was then that I began to experience an altogether unfamiliar and deeply unsettling type of injustice.

I could accept the fact Jews, Muslims, and Orthodox Christians would not welcome me. What I was unprepared for was the rejection by a significant portion of the Western church and its alarming silence about the ongoing human crisis playing out daily in the decidedly *un*-Holy Land.

Many American evangelical Christians cheered and applauded as nonbelieving Jewish authorities razed the homes of Palestinians, some of whom were their spiritual brothers and sisters in Christ. Millions of dollars from evangelical churches have been raised and distributed to build settlements on Palestinian land and arm its Jewish residents against their Arab neighbors.

When asked to help support Christian Arab churches, an overwhelming majority chose instead to continue to pour support into the secular nation of Israel. Eschatological interpretations—such as end-times theology—took precedence over every other biblical tenet, including the spread of the gospel.

Atrocity was constantly overlooked by many of my Western brothers and sisters in the pursuit of advancing the second coming of Christ. Arab believers largely were ignored and lumped in as "enemies of God's chosen people" because of their race.

Churches that regularly supported missions to nations around the globe bizarrely abandoned their support of mission to the Holy Land and concentrated instead on funding the very entities actively seeking to destroy the Christian presence in the land. How did this represent biblical justice? Or any type of justice?

Justice and unity in Jesus

I am a walking representation of the absurdity of the Holy Land. I am both Israeli and Palestinian. As a resident of the Holy Land, I am a physical recipient of the extraordinary legacy of the life of Jesus. But even more, as a follower of Christ, I am a spiritual recipient of the justice for which Jesus died and rose again.

Ironically, the very name under which we are called to unify has been used to endorse the worst discord. The land Jesus walked is a boiling cauldron of strife and injustice.

How can I truly seek justice? How can I encourage other believers to seek justice on behalf of my fellow Arabs?

The world is poised to unravel, and as the old falls away, I pray the new with which we replace it will be a better, stronger reflection of the truth we are called to represent. Only in unity with one another will we be able truly to seek justice.

R. E. works with Baptists in Texas as a cross-cultural mobilizer to equip churches for effective outreach. His full name is withheld due to security issues.

9

Justice looks like making things right
John D. Ogletree Jr.

I have been blessed to be the father of four wonderful children: three sons, all preachers—Johnny, Joseph, and Jordan—and one daughter, Lambreni.

Joseph and Jordan, the two youngest, are four years apart. During their upbringing, it was not uncommon for Joseph—who my wife described as an instigator—to take advantage of Jordan.

Jordan often came to me to intervene. What he sought without knowing it was justice. He needed me to "make it right," not just to acknowledge the wrong, sympathize, or pray. His entreaty was for me to use my authority and ability to "make it right."

That is what justice looks like to me—make it right.

Justice in the Old Testament

The Hebrew word used in the Old Testament over two hundred times for justice is *mishpat*. It is an attribute of God.

"Righteousness and justice are the foundation of your throne; mercy and truth go before your face" (Psalm 89:14).

Since justice is God's nature, he requires it of his people. "He has showed you, O man, what is good. And what does the Lord require of you? To act justly and to love mercy and to walk humbly with your God" (Micah 6:8).

Mishpat has several meanings in the Old Testament. Tim Keller, in *Generous Justice,* says: "Its most basic meaning is to treat people equitably. It means acquitting or punishing every person on the merits of the case, regardless of race or social status. . . . It is punishing wrongdoing as well as giving people their rights, and it is giving people what they are due."[1]

Four-hundred-year absence of justice

Jordan's youthful demand was symbolic of our times. In the aftermath of George Floyd's murder in Minneapolis, the cry for justice came across our nation from Black people, white people, Latinx, Asians, and Native Americans.

Demonstrations took place in over thirty cities, with signs that read, "Black Lives Matter," "No Justice No Peace," and "Liberty and Justice for ALL," demanding that America "make it right."

The time has come for our nation to reckon with the denial and lack of *mishpat* toward Black people, which commenced with the tenet of white supremacy that established a cruel, inhumane, and yes, sinful enslavement of Blacks brought from Africa lasting 246 years.

When slavery ended, those freed were denied justice through a system of "neo-slavery" through the Black Codes, betrayal during Reconstruction, the KKK, lynching, Jim Crow, segregation, and overt discrimination lasting another eighty-nine years.

The next period witnessed the end of segregation and the monumental Civil Rights Movement with its Civil Rights Act and Voting Rights Act. This period of 68 years perpetuated injustice with increased poverty, failed public education, housing discrimination, redlining, racial profiling, police brutality, mass incarceration, an unjust criminal justice system, gerrymandering, payday-loan establishments, voter suppression, poor health care, and the resurfacing of white supremacy. These periods total 403 years of justice denied.

What's expected of the church

When my son came seeking justice, it would have been wrong for me to tell him, "Get over it," or, "I do not want to hear anything about this," or, "I have not done anything to you." There can be no *mishpat* with indifference to suffering.

---

[1] Timothy Keller, *Generous Justice: How God's Grace Makes Us Just* (New York: Riverhead Books, 2010), 3–4.

In Old Testament Israel, every city had a gate where decisions were made for the welfare of its inhabitants. These decisions were economic, relational, and political. The overarching principal for all decisions was *mishpat*.

"Hate evil, and love good, and establish justice in the gate" (Amos 5:15).

The church of Jesus Christ should be the primary advocate for justice in America. Justice was a biblical concept before it became a political one. During this season of reflection and evaluation, the church can and should distinguish itself as a modern-day gate-keeper for what the last phrase in the Pledge of Allegiance promises: "liberty and justice for all."

A plan leading to justice

To be gatekeepers for *mishpat*, it is essential that the Baptist General Convention of Texas, along with its white pastors and churches, prioritize "making it right" and develop a plan that leads to justice.

1. Hold a summit on justice and racial equality.
2. Listen to, learn from, and love victims of injustice.
3. Preach on justice consistently—biblically, not politically.
4. Speak out against injustice whenever it occurs.
5. Partner with a Black church whose resources are substantially less than yours for kingdom expansion.
6. Partner with a public school whose student population is laden with poverty.
7. Practice justice throughout all organizations, establishing inclusion, diversity, equality, and equity as policy.
8. Pray for change.

Dr. John D. Ogletree Jr., senior pastor of First Metropolitan Church of Houston, has held many leadership roles with the executive board of the Baptist General Convention of Texas, including the presidency of the African American Fellowship of the BGCT and moderatorship of the Union Baptist Association. Dr. Ogletree was board president for the Cypress-Fairbanks Independent School District and served five terms as a board trustee.

10

Justice for immigrants and refugees seldom seen

Marv Knox

Justice looks like parents crying tears of joy because they no longer worry about daughters raped and sons conscripted into organized crime. It looks like the smile of a teacher realizing no one will kill her for helping someone learn to read.

Justice looks like the hands of a laborer who can provide for her family again. It looks like a head bowed in prayer, now free to follow the dictates of conscience.

Unfortunately, justice like this is difficult to glimpse—much less view in fullness—these days.

Justice looks like immigrants to the United States—allowed to seek asylum here because ours is a nation of immigrants. It looks like refugees who never intended to seek shelter within our borders, people who love their homelands. It looks like victims who fled extortion, rape, and murder.

Justice looks like bodies descended from generations of farmers whose livelihoods have been decimated by climate change. It looks like the worn knees of people who prayed long and hard before they fled to America. Justice looks like the happy faces of full-bellied children, safe beside their mamas and papas.

Looking harder for justice

You don't see justice like this as often as you used to. US government policy pushes it away. Once, people whose love for family compelled them to flee their homes could seek refuge in this country. They arrived legally, asking only to state their cases, receive fair hearings, and be granted asylum—safety, opportunity, justice.

In January 2019, the US Department of Homeland Security implemented the Migrant Protection Protocols—known as "Remain in Mexico."[1] The policy requires non-Mexican immigrants seeking asylum to wait out the process in Mexico, confined to some of the most dangerous cities in North America.

To make matters worse, US immigration officers' jobs changed. They switched from seeking to understand asylum seekers' stories—often involving abuse, oppression, and terror—to looking for the tiniest technical reason to thwart the asylum process. To slam shut the door of safety, opportunity, justice.

Injustice looks like mischaracterizing others

Asylum seekers have been maligned as rapists, thugs, gang members, and opportunists—people who want to come to the United States illegally, freeload off our country, and take Americans' jobs. While the thousands of people who seek US asylum may include a miniscule number of immigrants with malevolent intent, this is an outright lie about almost all the refugees seeking entrance into "the land of the free and the home of the brave."

They already are brave, and they seek freedom. What but love and courage would compel parents to uproot young families and leave home for a shot at living in a strange land?

Fellowship Southwest works alongside pastors all along the United States–Mexico border to provide food and shelter to asylum seekers who remain in Mexico. We know them. We know their stories. All things being equal, they would not have left their homelands unless they felt it was absolutely necessary.

Reasons for seeking asylum

They seek US asylum for various reasons, including the following:

- **Gangs**—organized criminals—rule their countries. Mothers bring their children because daughters have been raped and sons killed for refusing to join the

[1] https://www.dhs.gov/news/2019/01/24/migrant-protection-protocols.

gangs. Fathers bring their families because wanton violence has made providing for and protecting them impossible back home.

- **Extreme poverty** has made even mere subsistence impossible in their homelands. This isn't about greed and wanting bigger and better. Thousands of refugees come from families who have lived on and worked the land for generations. Agricultural degradation caused by climate change has robbed them of that privilege. They left so they could work even menial jobs to raise their children.

- **Persecution** has pushed them out. Some refugees come here because their minority religious faith has made them targets of abuse. Some come because their love for democracy has caused them to be considered "enemies" of their own countries. Some have been industrious, and their success—financially minor by US standards—made them victims of extortion.

These are decent, hard-working, kind people. Their industry and courage and belief in our country will translate not only into safety and security for themselves but into a stronger, braver, more resilient America.

The prophets taught us to care for and protect the stranger. Jesus said we demonstrate our love for him by how we treat "the least of these." If we do not seek immigration reform and a fair and open asylum process, we turn blind eyes toward justice.

Marv Knox was founding coordinator of Fellowship Southwest, a multicultural, ecumenical Cooperative Baptist Fellowship network across Arizona, New Mexico, northern Mexico, Oklahoma, Southern California, and Texas, from 2017 to 2021. He was editor of the Baptist Standard *from 1999 to 2017.*

11

Justice looks like hope, not hopelessness

Rev. Nell Green

Many of us have contemplated justice more in 2020 than we have perhaps in our entire lives. In these days of pandemic, striving for racial equality, and economic ruination, we are asking ourselves questions about justice and what constitutes justice. These are questions we should have asked long before now.

What is fair? What is valid? What is peace? What is genuine respect for others? What is right? What is wholeness? What is hope? What is justice?

Bryan Stevenson, author of *Just Mercy: A Story of Justice and Redemption*, stated, "I think hopelessness is the enemy of justice. I think injustice prevails where hopelessness persists."[1]

What hopelessness looks like

Bombs fall each day, and the older sister wonders if her siblings will come home that day from school. One by one, they leave their country, not knowing where they will go. Hopelessness.

The oppressive government strangled individual rights, so he spoke up. He was imprisoned. Hopelessness.

A gang showed up at her door and threatened to kill her entire family if they were not out of their house by the next day. They left. Hopelessness.

---

[1] https://www.3blmedia.com/news/trailblazer-takeaways-just-mercy -author-bryan-stevenson-achieving-equal-justice.

They live on about a dollar a day. When the pandemic crippled the economy, the absence of resources was immediate. Whole communities unable to feed their families. Hopelessness.

She has a PhD from an American university. Yet she fears going to purchase a movie ticket from the ticket booth because of how she is treated when she speaks with an accent. Hopelessness.

She was sexually abused as a child. At age fifteen, she did not think she was worthy of anything other than selling herself. There were those who preyed on that vulnerability. Her loss was their gain. Hopelessness.

He is willing to work and work hard. He wants to feed his family. Others capitalize on his desperation by forcing him to labor in their restaurants. Hopelessness.

Hope involves us

In Mark 2, we read of the paralyzed man. He was brought to Jesus for healing. The friends in this account sought wholeness, hope, peace, fairness, and more for their friend. We find here actions we can imitate so we, too, can be instruments of justice.

In verse 3, we read, "Some people arrived, and four of them were bringing to him a man who was paralyzed."

"Some people." Only four were carrying him, but there were more than these four who sought what was right and fair for the paralyzed man.

It will take our collective action and our collective commitment for justice to prevail. The paralyzed man could not seek wholeness for himself. It took not one, two, three, or four, but *some* people.

A pastor friend of mine recently pointed out there are no gender designations here. People brought him to Jesus.

What compelled these people to bring this man to a crowded room? What was their plan? What were their hopes?

We are the hands, feet, and mouths of justice for those who are "paralyzed." Too many are not able to seek justice. We seek it for them.

This group worked together to help the paralyzed man have the opportunity for wholeness. We must do it together in harmony and unity. Hope, not hopelessness.

Hope involves access

In verse 4, we read, "They couldn't carry him through the crowd, so they tore off part of the roof above where Jesus was."

Access is life. Whether it is racial equality, economic stability, health care, gender, age vulnerability, education, safe drinking water, peaceful communities—without access, change cannot occur.

This is one of the most obvious disparities of recent months—those who have access and those who do not.

Not everyone has had access to health, equality, or protection from economic ruin. As each of us experiences these turbulent times, we have been forced to realize fragility is no respecter of persons.

Stability, strength, and healing come with access to systems of justice. These friends knew the paralyzed man needed to get to Jesus. They had to think creatively and make some very bold moves.

It was bold to think they could get the man there. It was bold to think they could get him up on the roof. It was extremely bold to cut a hole in the roof. It was bold to lower the man in front of Jesus, demanding Jesus give this man the attention they knew he deserved. Hope, not hopelessness.

Hope involves faith

Verse 5 says Jesus saw their faith. He saw the faith of the friends and said to the paralytic, "Your sins are forgiven."

Grace and mercy were extended to the one paralyzed because the friends had faith. Faith that their friend would experience justice and wholeness. Faith that Jesus would act. Faith that healing would occur.

They had the kind of faith that picks up the one unable and goes above and beyond to see access is gained. Hope, not hopelessness.

What does justice look like? It looks like hope.

How are we to counter the hopelessness that is the enemy of justice? By working together in harmony and unity, by acting creatively with boldness and with faith, justice will occur.

Rev. Nell Green served as a career missionary in Dakar, Senegal; Miami; North and South Carolina; and Brussels, Belgium.

She also served with the Cooperative Baptist Fellowship in Houston, ministering to the needs of refugees—helping them resettle and providing educational programs and social entrepreneurship—and partnered with various agencies to raise awareness about and prevent human trafficking. Before retiring in July 2023, she served CBF as the Offering for Global Missions Advocate.

12

Justice looks like the kingdom of God

Albert L. Reyes

Justice at its core is treating people in a right way, an ethical and honest way.

Justice under the law is when judges, lawyers, and law enforcement officers treat an accused person with dignity and respect.

Justice in the workplace means everyone is treated without partiality, as a person created in the image of God with incredible potential.

Justice in a social context means we relate and organize through institutions, organizations, and social structures in a just manner. It means everyone influenced or impacted by those systems experiences dignity, respect, and being regarded as one created in the image of God.

The opposite of justice is injustice, the absence of justice in any individual, institutional, or relational context. A lack of justice inevitably exists due to the presence of sin. So, in one sense, we cannot escape injustice because we are all sinners.

Prejudice, racism, discrimination, power, control, influence, superiority, jealousy, envy, wrath, pride, and an inventory of sins are recorded by the Apostle Paul in his letter to the church at Ephesus (Ephesians 4:20–5:21). He instructs us to become imitators of God, living a life of love and reflecting the love of Christ for sinners like you and me.

Escaping injustice requires transformation

The only way to escape the habit of sin and our innate gravitational pull toward injustice is through a radical transformation of our minds (Romans 12:2). Do not miss this. How you think is what you do.

Rather than being conformed to the type of this world, Paul calls us to be transformed by the renewing of our minds. This is the work of the Holy Spirit in us as we allow him to shape our hearts and minds freely. This is the pragmatic birthplace of justice for us in our hearts and minds.

Justice, in a Christian context, happens when we think like Jesus did. You may think it is impossible to think this way, "but we have the mind of Christ," Paul contends in 1 Corinthians 2:16.

Rediscovering the kingdom

I was totally stunned while doing research for my recent book, *Hope Now: Peace, Healing, and Justice When the Kingdom Comes Near*, at the Oxford Centre for Mission Studies in Oxford, England, during the summer of 2017.

I rediscovered Matthew 6:33 while digging deeper into the meaning of the kingdom of God. I learned the Septuagint (Greek translation of the Hebrew Old Testament) translated the concept of "righteousness" as "justice," which is also captured in the sixteenth-century Reina Valera translation of the Bible into Spanish.

A new rendering of this verse would be "Seek first the kingdom of God and the justice of God, and all these things will be added to you."

Justice was not something I pursued as a priority. I understood I should chase the kingdom of God, but not necessarily his justice. Pursuing the righteousness of God meant pursuing him but not uniquely prioritizing his justice. That may seem like a silly or insignificant nuance. However, for me, this was revolutionary.

Above all things, Jesus challenges us to seek his kingdom, his reign, and his justice. Did he not teach his disciples to pray in this way: "Thy kingdom come; thy will be done on earth as it is in heaven?"

What the kingdom of God looks like

For the kingdom of God and the justice of God to come near to us means we would know each other better, especially across ethno-racial and cultural identities; we habitually would treat each other with dignity and respect; we would lead rather than follow society on issues of racial inequality.

Our congregations and institutional ministries would reflect a multicultural, multiracial, and multiethnic fabric of identity at all levels of leadership. If the kingdom came near to us, we would see cultural and ethnic diversity in membership, staffing, leadership, volunteers, and senior leadership and on our boards.

When the King and his kingdom came near in the early church, power and control of resources, authority, and leadership were shared, and the Lord increased their number. The church would not have grown from five hundred disciples to more than three million in the first three centuries had they not overcome the proclivity toward monocultural identity, power, and control of resources.

The early church actively answered this question: What is the best way to live life on the planet? This is the twenty-first-century question up for debate in our families, our communities, our congregations, our institutions, our nation, and our world.

We know the Jesus way is the answer. Yet the gap between what we know and what we do remains deep and wide.

Dr. Albert L. Reyes is president and CEO of Buckner International.

13

Justice is making sure Black lives matter

Patricia Wilson

Three hundred years ago, in what would become America, it was not a crime to kill a slave who was undergoing "correction." Black lives didn't matter.

One hundred years ago, lynching—another name for premeditated conspiracy to murder—rarely was prosecuted, and in those few instances where it was, acquittal essentially was guaranteed. Black lives didn't matter.

Sixty years ago, members of the Ku Klux Klan could kidnap, torture, or murder civil rights activists or even innocent individuals, like the four little girls of the 16th Avenue Baptist Church in Birmingham, Alabama, sometimes with the complicity of local law enforcement officials. There was scant concern of prosecution or conviction. That a few murderers were convicted in later years does not alter the fact that terrorizing African Americans and their allies was a low-risk crime. Black lives didn't matter.

And let's not forget that since 1619, when the first Africans were traded as commodities, and carrying through to the 1950s, rape of Black women seldom was punished, notwithstanding overwhelming evidence of the crime. Indeed, sexual assault of Black women seemingly was accepted. The 1944 case of Recy Taylor, gang-raped by six white men who never were prosecuted, is just one case in point. At the same time, Black men could be lynched and Black communities destroyed at the mere suggestion of sexual impropriety involving a white woman. Black women's lives didn't matter.

Then and now

Today one need only list the names recently in the news and reflect objectively on the justice system's response to the various incidents to begin to understand why the Black Lives Matter movement resonates in the African American community.

Ahmaud Arbery's life mattered little to the three white men who are charged with murdering him. Their bias against Black people led them to believe Arbery to be a burglary suspect, and that was justification enough for them to dispense their vigilante "justice." That Arbery was unarmed and seemingly engaged in nothing more than an afternoon jog initially sparked no arrests or even a thorough investigation by the original district attorney who reviewed the case. Arbery's life didn't matter.

Trayvon Martin's life mattered little to George Zimmerman, who shot the seventeen-year-old, who was walking home after purchasing a snack and a soft drink. Nor did it matter much to the jury that acquitted Zimmerman. Pursuant to Florida's "stand your ground" legislation, Zimmerman was not required to retreat from the unarmed child he assaulted; he could use deadly force even though he instigated the altercation with the teenager. Trayvon Martin had no right to stand his ground; his life didn't matter.

George Floyd's life seemingly mattered little to Derek Chauvin, the police officer seen kneeling on Floyd's neck for nearly nine minutes, his hands nonchalantly stuffed in his pockets as Floyd's life seeped from his body. Nor did it seemingly matter to the other three officers on the scene who did little to protect Floyd.

As for me

Raised by Christian parents and educated in parochial school, I learned we are wonderfully made in the image of God. I was taught we all are children of God.

As a lawyer, I firmly believe in the directive of Micah 6:8, that we all are called to act justly, to love mercy, and to walk humbly with our God.

So, what does justice look like to me? It does not mean ignoring differences. It does, however, mean being ever sensitive to implicit biases that too often blind us to the insignificance of those differences based on race or skin color.

Just as importantly, justice looks like acknowledging explicit racism and addressing it rather than deflecting to other issues to excuse the problem. For example, Black-on-Black crime is an issue, but it diminishes in no way that police brutality disproportionately affects African Americans or that statistics show Blacks are more likely than whites to be arrested on suspicion of the same crime and are more likely to be given harsher sentences if convicted as compared to whites.

Justice means really and truly leaning into Dr. Martin Luther King Jr.'s dream that we judge a man by the content of his character rather than the color of his skin. The closer we come to doing that, the more we can boldly and proudly proclaim a just society in which all lives really do matter.

Patricia Wilson is a lawyer and a member of the Baylor Law School faculty, teaching courses in employment law and family law. She has served as moderator of the Cooperative Baptist Fellowship.

14

Justice looks like tearing down the wall between you and Christ

Bethany Rivera Molinar

I was born, raised, and now live in El Paso. El Paso is a great place to live if you like to run, and I do. My runs regularly take me up to a place where I can see all three cities and states that adjoin each other here.

A few weeks ago, while on a morning run on my usual route, I noticed two things at a distance I hadn't realized could be seen from my vantage point.

To the left of my viewpoint was a thick black line in stark contrast to the natural colors of the desert landscape. This is a part of the border wall funded by private donations.

Directly across and above this wall is Mount Cristo Rey, which sits on both sides of the international border between the United States and Mexico. The mountain is named for the statue of Christ located at its top.

The figure of Christ stands in front of a giant cross. His eyes gaze out over the borderland, and his arms are outstretched with his palms facing outward over three cities and two nations.

As I thought about this picture—a manmade barrier created to keep people out directly across from a statue of Jesus on Mount Cristo Rey—Christ's words came to my mind: "For I was hungry, and you gave me nothing to eat, I was thirsty and you gave me nothing to drink, I was a stranger and you did not invite me in. . . . Truly I tell you, whatever you did not do for the least of these, you did not do for me" (Matthew 25:42–43, 45).

Caring for Christ at our border

Over the past few years, our city has been center stage to a humanitarian crisis. We have had front row seats as thousands of asylum seekers have traveled north to seek refuge at our border.

Our brothers and sisters seeking asylum shared with us their stories of what pushed them out of their beloved homelands and stories of the perilous journey that led them to our churches and nonprofits. Their journeys were fraught with danger on their way to the United States.

They also told of the harsh conditions they faced at the hands of federal agents and facilities after they surrendered themselves at our border.

Christ himself arrived at our doors. Churches, nonprofit organizations, and individuals in our city responded to his knocking by working together to provide these brothers and sisters with shelter—a place to rest and catch their breath before waiting for their court hearings.

We gave them a clean set of clothes. We fed them. We prayed with them, and they prayed over us. Through this experience, we were ministered to in sanctifying, paradigm-shifting ways through the binding of the Holy Spirit between us and our brothers and sisters.

Christ came to our border. It was tough work. We were stretched thin. But we were motivated by a holy calling to love our neighbors as ourselves.

Caring for our brothers and sisters

When the Remain in Mexico policy was enacted, Christ was barred from crossing the border as thousands of asylum seekers were forced to wait for their court hearings for several months in Mexico.

Our brothers and sisters in Mexico responded by opening their doors to their neighbors seeking asylum. They fed them. They clothed them. They gave them shelter. And they continue to minister to many who have nowhere else to turn.

These ministers to Christ are stretched thin. They have become vulnerable to danger from gangs who do not want these churches to provide refuge to asylum seekers. But they still serve, sharing what little resources they may have because they are compelled by their faith to love their neighbor as themselves—to love and serve Christ, who has come knocking at their door.

Walling Christ out

Through a concerted effort by our government, a wall has been placed between us and our brothers and sisters seeking asylum. This wall is physical, but it also is legal, spiritual, emotional.

Our brothers and sisters are returned—by the planeload and in the dead of night—to their home countries, where they face certain danger. They have been kept in subhuman conditions and incarcerated for indefinite amounts of time while awaiting their fate.

Their children have been ripped from their arms, scarred, and traumatized by the separation of their primary source of comfort and refuge. They have been denied the universally recognized human right of seeking asylum.

When you create a divide that prevents people from seeking refuge—be it through a literal, physical wall or a policy or by choosing consciously to do nothing in response to the cries of your brothers and sisters—you also put up a wall between you and Christ.

Your justification for that divide may be fear, a love of country over and above Christ's command to love your neighbor as yourself, ignorance, or racism. But still, the wall remains, and you separate yourself from Christ.

"Whatever you did not do for the least of these, you did not do for me," Jesus said. "Depart from me" (Matthew 25:41, 45).

Letting Christ in

But Christ—whose ways are higher and holier than any manmade barrier—stands atop the holy mountain. His eyes are gazing outward toward you beyond the wall you've built between you and him. His hands are reaching outward, ready to reconcile you to him. But you have to tear down that wall.

Take heart; have courage. Trust and obey God and tear down the oppressive manmade structures—be they physical barriers or policies that keep out those who are vulnerable.

Until you do, you wall out Christ.

"Truly, I say to you, as you did it to one of the least of these my brothers, you did it to me" (Matthew 25:40).

Bethany Rivera Molinar serves as the executive director of Ciudad Nueva Community Outreach and has served as the president of the Texas Christian Community Development Network. She lives, works, and worships in her downtown neighborhood in El Paso with her husband, Adrian, and their three children.

15

Three ways justice looks like Jesus
Patty Lane

Money changers in the temple

Justice looks like a standing up for what is right regardless of who it might offend.

In Mark 11:15–17, we learn of Jesus driving out the money changers from the temple. This event is about so much more than pigeons sold in the courtyard.

It is about Jesus seeing the injustice created in order that some would profit unfairly at the expense of others. It was a reaction to the plight of the faithful, who only wanted to fulfill the law, and how the greed of others was stealing that from them.

Jesus could not let that stand. He could not know and do nothing. He had to call out their sin and stop them.

Justice looks like that. It looks like the courage to call out what is wrong and to work to make it stop no matter the consequence.

The Pharisees and the woman

Justice looks like treating people with dignity no matter who they are and what is in their past.

In John 8:1–11, John tells us of the Pharisees and the teachers of the law bringing to Jesus a woman caught in adultery. Scripture says they did this to trap him. With the appearance of wanting justice, those leaders also were using this woman for their own agenda.

Jesus' focus was on what was best for the woman. Unlike the others, Jesus would not use her, for that is the opposite of justice.

Jesus immediately looked down so as not to look on the woman, who may not have been totally clothed. When he spoke, it was to her accusers. Rather than judging her, he asked the men who brought her to look at their own lives. When there was no one left to stone her, then Jesus said, "Go, and sin no more."

Is that justice? Should she have been punished?

For Jesus, justice began with empathy and love. Then he focused on setting things right, making clear the path so what should have happened could happen. Jesus knew what we do not know about this woman. In his justice, he released her to go and live the life she was meant to live.

The hungry crowd

Justice looks like compassion.

In Mark 6:34–44, Jesus had compassion on the crowd because he saw they were like sheep without a shepherd and were hungry. His disciples seemed annoyed. They went with Jesus to eat and rest, but the crowd followed. Jesus' compassion cost the disciples their rest and their meal.

The disciples thought Jesus would send the crowd away when they got hungry, but Jesus had another plan. He asked his disciples to feed them. This really must have irritated them. They even asked, "Are we supposed to go and buy bread and give it to them?"

How was that fair? They had not invited the crowds to join them.

Does Jesus' compassion ever annoy us or inconvenience us? How many times have we thought, "Surely God does not want me to speak out—or feed, house, be there, or share."

Maybe we think, "It is not my responsibility. I did not cause this problem. It's too big. There's nothing I can do that will make a difference."

That is the thing about Jesus' justice. We often do not want to be a part of it. Jesus could have left the disciples with their own solutions—buying food or sending the crowd away hungry. But Jesus had another way and a lesson to teach.

Justice is about who God is

Being compassionate is not about resources or swooping in like a superhero. It is not about us at all. It's not even about the other person. Being compassionate is about who God is.

Jesus wanted the crowd fed because of who he is. He wanted the disciples to learn whatever they have, when placed in God's hands, is always more than enough.

We often think of justice as getting what is deserved. But Jesus' justice is about getting better than we deserve. The gospel message is we are sinners, and through no goodness on our part, Jesus came and died so we could have eternal life. Better than we deserve, right?

His justice is that way, too. His justice says we speak up for those who cannot. We treat others—all others—with dignity and offer a way out. We show compassion even when it is costly.

Justice looks like Jesus. The question is, Do we look like Jesus?

Patty Lane retired as director of intercultural ministries for the Baptist General Convention of Texas.

16

Justice looks like being willing to be uncomfortable
Mariah Humphries

It was the morning of July 9, 2020.

I kept refreshing the *SCOTUSblog* webpage. A decision *had* to be today. Suddenly, my eyes welled up and a lump formed in my throat.

I sat there for several seconds, attempting to swallow, processing what my eyes were taking in. When I finally could speak, my fist raised in the air, I looked at my husband, who was casually drinking his morning coffee. The only words I could say were, "We won!"

The Supreme Court affirmed part of eastern Oklahoma remained Native American land. Specifically, it remained the land of the Mvskoke—commonly known as the Muscogee (Creek) Nation, my tribal nation.

This decision is important to the collective Native community. It showed the nation *we are still here*.

I prayed in the following minutes and thanked God for a piece of justice being served:

- Justice for the constant battle against invisibility as a people yet hypervisualization as a culture.
- Justice for a people forced to leave their own land through the Indian Removal Act in 1836, led by President Andrew Jackson.
- Justice for the resiliency of a people to adapt and thrive with unfamiliar soil and terrain.
- Justice for being stripped of that new land by the Treaty of 1866.

Recognizing injustice

To recognize justice, we first must know the face of injustice. I find injustice is nurtured and maintained when we focus on centering ourselves and our comfort. Within Christianity, comfort too often is projected as theology or doctrine. The Bible becomes the weapon to protect our preference over the truth. In order to be the hands of Jesus, the opposite must occur. We must become selfless and focus on the well-being of those around us.

Discomfort can result in un-Christian reactions, which must be resolved through confession and repentance so love, kindness, and humility can thrive and ultimately heal through justice.

What could be lacking in our pursuit for justice? Gary Vanderpol, in *Return to Justice*, has a straightforward statement about Christians and justice. "Too often [we] choose justice issues that [we] feel do not implicate [ourselves] so that [we] can play the heroic role of rescuer."

We are pro-justice up to the point where we have been unjust. For example, when it comes to racial injustice, our money, votes, and our social media posts tend to confirm what Vanderpol presents. We support the areas we feel cannot implicate us among the guilty. Once we enter areas of guilt, we stand by preference, not truth.

Symbolic vs. true sorrow

Although many showed support for the Muscogee over the years in their pursuit for the right to have their land, the focus ultimately was not on the Muscogees' welfare. When the US Supreme Court decision was announced, concern immediately switched to the impact on the non-Natives living on Native land and the economic result for Oklahoma.

This switch in concern revealed much of the support received was individual and, as Sarah Deer—university distinguished professor at the University of Kansas and herself Mvskoke—calls it, "symbolic sorrow" rather than a true desire for justice for Native Americans.

I often hear phrases like "This all takes time" or "Justice is happening. It has to go through the process." I usually hear these types of responses from white Christian sisters and brothers who tend to benefit from injustice toward others.

Raymond Chang, from the Asian American Christian Collaborative, shares an important step in justice work.

"The burden can't always be on people of color to be patient and endure when the changes that need to be made aren't that complicated," Chang writes. "At some point, people need to start taking responsibility for the inequities they perpetrate—whether or not they themselves fully comprehend it."

For me, justice looks like being the hands and feet of Christ. That means I may become uncomfortable, challenged, and dismissed. To pursue justice means I stay in those moments and keep moving forward because it is not my preference at work, but God's truth.

What does justice look like for you?

Mariah Humphries (M.T.S.) is a Mvskoke Nation citizen, writer, and educator. Through her experience navigating the tension between Native and white American culture, she brings Native awareness to non-Native spaces. With over twenty years of vocational ministry service, she is focused on theology and racial literacy within the American church.

17

Justice looks like a divine invitation

Nora O. Lozano

For me, justice looks like a divine invitation from God to join in the coming of God's reign here on Earth. In the introduction to this series, Eric Black invited us to see justice as "central to God's character and God's interaction with creation." Furthermore, Black affirms, "When creation is unjust, the Creator will make sure justice is accomplished."

As part of God's attributes, justice is one of the standards God has set before us as human beings. In his book *Introducing Christian Doctrine*, theologian Millard Erickson highlights, "God expects his followers to emulate his righteousness and justice. We are to adopt as our standard his law and precepts. We are to treat others fairly and justly because that is what God himself does."[1]

While it is true justice is more than an invitation—it is God's requirement for our lives (Micah 6:8)—I like to see it as an invitation. God does not force us to be just but gives us an opportunity to choose to do the right thing.

It is an invitation to join our Creator, as Black mentioned, in making sure justice is accomplished. If accepted, this invitation will get us closer to fulfilling our purpose of giving glory to God.

Gifted to enact justice

As we are invited to join God in this project of building God's reign here on earth, we are not invited empty-handed. The Holy

[1]   Millard Erickson, *Introducing Christian Doctrine*, ed. L. Arnold Hustad, 2nd ed. (Grand Rapids: Baker Academic, 2001), 101.

Spirit, based on God's will and his own choosing, has graced us with different gifts (1 Corinthians 12:11, 18). Often, these gifts are correlated with the areas of passion God has placed in our hearts.

Together, these gifts and areas of passion are part of God's invitation to join in a particular area of God's concern where justice needs to be accomplished.

In my particular case, the Holy Spirit has graced me with the gift of teaching through spoken and written words. I have spent more than twenty-five years encouraging students, especially minority ones, to open their imaginations to a broader and richer future through the wonderful world of knowledge and education.

At Baptist University of the Américas, I have encouraged them to believe they can finish college and continue to graduate school. I have been teaching at BUA for twenty years, long enough to have the blessing of witnessing the success of former students as they graduate with their masters and doctorates.

My hope is these former students, in turn, will continue encouraging other minority students in such a way that God's justice is accomplished in our communities.

Latina leadership

Another area where God has invited me to join in this project of accomplishing justice is the one of women's issues. The fact I am a Latina woman with a doctorate opens the imagination of minority women and encourages them to study and obtain the highest academic degrees. When they see me, they may think, "If she, as a Latina, was able to do it, I can do it, too."

Additionally, God has invited me to join in this task of accomplishing justice through the work of the Christian Latina Leadership Institute, where the goal is to train women in leadership issues—personal and professional/ministerial—in order to become agents of transformation in their families, churches, and communities. As they become agents of transformation, they also join in God's project of accomplishing justice in their communities.

To think God invites me every day to join in accomplishing God's justice and developing his reign here on earth is a privilege, a responsibility, and a joy.

You're invited, too

In the same way, God also is inviting you to join in this project of accomplishing justice and developing his reign.

What are your areas of passion? What are your gifts? Whatever they are, God has given them to you with the purpose of inviting you to join in a particular area where justice needs to be accomplished.

Today there are so many areas where justice is needed. Let's listen to God's invitation. Let's find our place in the service of God's reign. Let's bring honor and glory to God through just and right actions.

Dr. Nora O. Lozano is professor of theological studies at Baptist University of the Américas and executive director of the Christian Latina Leadership Institute in San Antonio, Texas.

La justicia es como una invitación divina
Nora O. Lozano

Para mí, la justicia es como una invitación divina de parte de Dios a participar en la venida de su reino aquí en la Tierra. En la introducción a esta serie, Eric Black nos invitó a ver a la justicia como "fundamental para el carácter de Dios y la interacción de Dios con el mundo." Además, Black afirma, "Cuando la creación es injusta, el Creador se asegurará de que se cumpla la justicia."

Como parte de los atributos de Dios, la justicia es uno de los estándares que Dios ha establecido ante nosotros como seres humanos. En su libro *Introducing Christian Doctrine*, el teólogo Millard Erickson destaca, "Dios espera que sus seguidores emulen su rectitud y justicia. Debemos adoptar como norma su ley y preceptos. Debemos tratar a las demás personas de manera justa y equitativa porque eso mismo es lo que Dios hace."[2]

---

[2]   Millard Erickson, *Introducing Christian Doctrine*, ed. L. Arnold Hustad, 2nd ed. (Grand Rapids: Baker Academic, 2001), 101.

Si bien es cierto que la justicia es más que una invitación, pues es un requisito de Dios para nuestras vidas (Miqueas 6:8), a mí me gusta verla como una invitación. Dios no nos obliga a ser personas justas, sino que nos da la oportunidad de elegir hacer lo correcto.

Es una invitación a unirse a nuestro Creador, como mencionó Black, para asegurarnos de que se haga justicia. Si la aceptamos, esta invitación nos acercará más al cumplimiento de nuestro propósito de darle gloria a Dios.

Dotados para hacer justicia

Cuando recibimos la invitación a unirnos a Dios en este proyecto de construir su reino aquí en la tierra, no se nos invita con las manos vacías. El Espíritu Santo, basado en la voluntad de Dios y su propia elección, nos ha dotado con diferentes dones (1 Corintios 12:11, 18). A menudo, estos dones están relacionados con las áreas de pasión que Dios ha puesto en nuestros corazones.

Juntos, estos dones y áreas de pasión son parte de la invitación de Dios a unirnos en un área particular que le interesa a Dios, donde se debe de alcanzar justicia.

En mi caso particular, el Espíritu Santo me ha dado el don de enseñar a través de la palabra hablada y escrita. He pasado más de 25 años animando a estudiantes, especialmente a quienes pertenecen a grupos minoritarios, a abrir su imaginación a un futuro más vasto y rico a través del maravilloso mundo del conocimiento y la educación.

En la Universidad Bautista de las Américas (Baptist University of the Américas), les he animado a creer que pueden terminar la universidad y continuar con estudios de posgrado. He estado enseñando en BUA durante 20 años, tiempo suficiente para tener la bendición de presenciar el éxito de exalumnos/as a medida que se gradúan de sus maestrías y doctorados.

Mi esperanza es que estos antiguos estudiantes, a su vez, continúen alentando a otros estudiantes de grupos minoritarios, de tal manera que la justicia de Dios se alcance en nuestras comunidades.

Latinas en liderazgo

Otra área en la que Dios me ha invitado a unirme a este proyecto de hacer justicia es la de las mujeres. El hecho de ser una mujer latina con un doctorado, abre la imaginación de las mujeres de grupos minoritarios, y las anima a estudiar y a obtener los más altos títulos académicos. Al verme, ellas pueden pensar, "Si ella, como latina, pudo hacerlo, yo también puedo hacerlo."

Además, Dios me ha invitado a unirme a esta tarea de alcanzar justicia a través del trabajo del Instituto Cristiano para Líderes Latinas (Christian Latina Leadership Institute), donde la meta es capacitar a las mujeres en asuntos de liderazgo, personal y profesional/ministerial, para que se conviertan en agentes de transformación en sus familias, iglesias y comunidades. A medida que se convierten en agentes de transformación, ellas también se unen al proyecto de Dios de alcanzar justicia en sus comunidades.

Pensar que Dios me invita todos los días a unirme a este proyecto de alcanzar su justicia y extender su reino aquí en la tierra, es un privilegio, una responsabilidad y un gozo.

La invitación es para usted también

De la misma forma, Dios también le invita a usted a unirse a este proyecto de hacer justicia y desarrollar el Reino.

¿Cuáles son sus áreas de pasión? ¿Cuáles son sus dones? Cualesquiera que sean, Dios se los ha dado con el propósito de invitarle a unirse en un área en particular donde se debe alcanzar justicia.

Hoy en día hay muchas áreas donde se necesita justicia. Escuchemos la invitación de Dios. Encontremos nuestro lugar al servicio del reino de Dios. Démosle el honor y la gloria a Dios mediante acciones justas y rectas.

La Dra. Nora O. Lozano es profesora de estudios teológicos en la Universidad Bautista de las Américas (Baptist University of the Américas) y directora ejecutiva del Instituto Cristiano para Líderes Latinas (Christian Latina Leadership Institute) en San Antonio, Texas.

18

Justice looks like being free of worry

Diego Silva

When I was thirteen years old, my parents set my sister, brother, and me in our small living room and told us we were moving to the United States. That news came as a big shock to us, even though many of our family members already had left Brazil in the 1990s to pursue a better life in other countries.

I did not know it then, but my parents—like many others—were faced with the task of making major decisions every day just to survive.

My parent's decision was based on a strong commitment to provide for their family and rested on the reality that freedom to seek a better life is intertwined with a commitment to justice—specifically, the ability to choose what the life of their family should look like.

Furthermore, it speaks to the incredible number of life-altering decisions vulnerable families must make every day.

Poverty affects life choices

Some of the challenges brought on by the poverty my parents faced on a daily basis included deciding between paying the rent or utility bills for the month and the ability to buy fresh meat and vegetables. They even found themselves faced with the decisions of which of their children would attend school and who would stay home. This is the reality for most people living in poverty.

Much research has been conducted in the areas of poverty and decision making.[1] Researchers agree people living in poverty make

[1] https://www.lse.ac.uk/PBS/Research/Research-Articles/How-poverty-affects-peoples-decision-making-processes.

many more life-altering and complex decisions compared to those with higher socioeconomic status.

This reality creates a life characterized by high levels of stress, social exclusion, lower confidence, and many other negative conditions that impact the psychology and physiological brain structures of people living in poverty.

Poverty along the border

Besides my own experiences with poverty, I have had a front-row seat to the impact poverty has on vulnerable families. For the last seven years, I have served with Buckner International on the Texas-Mexico border, working closely with vulnerable families in the Rio Grande Valley to strengthen them through education on finances, job skills, parenting, and more. We have helped numerous families open their first checking and savings accounts or implement their first budget.

The coronavirus pandemic has exacerbated the levels of stress vulnerable families have experienced lately. As parents lost their jobs, they were faced with the harsh reality of figuring out how to support their families. As schools closed, parents became educators. As days became weeks and weeks became months, the pressure and stress of the future led to an increase in child neglect and domestic abuse.[2]

Although we collectively have experienced higher levels of stress, the reality is my socioeconomic status and privilege have provided me a safety net many vulnerable families do not have. This has led me to believe justice is not only about "just behavior or treatment"; it also is about the privilege of not having to make life-altering decisions constantly.

Justice in light of our status

In its most simplistic and practical form, justice means I am able to write this piece, and you are able to read it without having to worry about how we will put healthy food on our tables tonight.

As people of faith, and as people with strong social justice convictions, we must use our privileged statuses to build a more equitable and loving world for those for whom "the long arc of the moral

[2] https://www.texastribune.org/2020/03/27/texas-coronavirus-child-abuse-likely-rise-risk/.

universe" has not yet "bent towards justice," to quote Dr. Martin Luther King Jr.

Justice also means we design programs that take the perspective of the people we are trying to help. As explained in a Chicago Booth Review research article,[3] we must be diligent to avoid designing programs that would appeal to people with the luxury to devote careful thought and attention in their consideration because "poverty imposes a heavy attentional 'tax' that prevents people from devoting that kind of thought to new opportunities."

Although my parents had to sacrifice so much to give my siblings and me a better life, I understand now that even then they had a moral responsibility to stand up and stand out for justice.

They taught us that no matter the circumstance, we always had a responsibility to make decisions that would build the kingdom of God instead of our own kingdoms. Ultimately, that is the one thing God will ask of us when we see him face-to-face.

Diego Silva is Director of Strategic Projects at Buckner International. He also serves as Board President of the Texas Christian Community Development Network, as Board Vice Chair of EduK Child Strategies, and as an academic coach in the Master of Public Administration program at the University of Texas Rio Grande Valley. He has completed a two-year fellowship at the USDA Center for Faith and Opportunity.

---

[3] https://review.chicagobooth.edu/behavioral-science/2018/article/how-poverty-changes-your-mind-set.

19

Images of justice in an emperor's land

Rev. Dr. Joseph C. Parker Jr.

Four images come to mind when I think about what justice looks like.

One is the statue Lady Justice.

Her blindfold, not part of her design until the sixteenth century, represents impartiality and objectivity, also depicted by a set of scales symbolizing the weight of a matter's strengths and weaknesses. An unsheathed sword indicates transparent and swift enforcement.

Another is from the 1837 Danish short story "The Emperor's New Clothes." Two swindlers arrive at the capital city of a vain emperor who spends lavishly on clothing at the state's expense, primarily concerned about the people's applause and showing off his new clothes.

Posing as weavers, they offer to supply him with magnificent clothes that are invisible to the stupid or incompetent. He proudly accepts, and his courtiers and the townspeople uncomfortably go along with the pretense, not wanting to appear foolish. But in the end they do.

The weavers mime dressing him in his new suit. He moves into a procession. A child blurts out that the emperor is naked, exposing him before everyone. The people then realize everyone has been fooled. Although startled about his nakedness, the emperor ever more proudly continues his procession.

A third image is depicted by those who live embracing Chris Marshall's description in *The Little Book of Biblical Justice*: "At the broadest level, then, justice entails the exercise of legitimate power to ensure that benefits and penalties are distributed fairly and equitably in society, thus meeting the rights and enforcing the obligations of all parties."[1]

The last looks like Jesus with his followers today on a journey, recognizing they must do justly, love mercy, and walk humbly with their God.

Jesus' followers in an emperor's land

I see them in an emperor's land in which God has willed just systems, structures, and institutions into existence for his purposes and the good and well-being of his creation so it will not devolve into chaos given humanity's fallen condition.

They arrive at various justice destination points; seeing justice is not about being nice or not, hateful or not.

They see the systems, structures, and institutions as God's prodigals, out of control. Their moral values—embedded in them by the people who designed, established, and worked in them—have lost their way. Their systems, structures, and institutions are sinful, distorted, biased, corrupt, oppressive, discriminatory, and exploitative because sinful people administer and operate them.

When sin accumulates among the land's people, their systems, structures, and institutions become overwhelmed and possessed by such sin because of their interrelatedness. This sources systemic injustice and is our reality.

But in Christ, this has been disarmed and defeated (Colossians 2:15).

Seeing justice in practice

I then see Jesus and his followers traveling. They are on a mission, recognizing—regardless of race, ethnicity, nationality, or gender—they are preaching good news to the poor; healing the brokenhearted; proclaiming liberty to the captives, incarcerated, brutalized, improperly segregated, and oppressed; and restoring the sight to the blind who are living among those and within out-of-control contexts.

---

[1] Chris Marshall, *The Little Book of Biblical Justice: A Fresh Approach to the Bible's Teachings on Justice* (Intercourse, Pa.: Good Books, 2005).

I see them stopping for beggars like Bartimaeus—who need relief from food insecurity, food deserts, lending, payday loans, and other oppressive systems—as Jesus asks, "What do you want me to do for you?" (Matthew 20:32). For they recognize justice is not "just for us."

They see misused, pained, and mistreated people because of disparities of power, privilege, race, ethnicity, gender, and money. They clearly see the emperor is naked as he exercises power, distributes benefits and penalties, and enforces rights and obligations.

They compassionately hear the cries, complaints, and crises of people who are harassed, helpless, and sick and who need health care and allies.

They embrace South Africa's Bishop Desmond Tutu's words, "If you are neutral in situations of injustice, you have chosen the side of the oppressor."

They act, protest, and intervene—challenging policies and practices of the out-of-control systems—to remove and "loose the chains of injustice" (Isaiah 58:6).

Confronting the emperor

They confront the fragile emperor, who shows discomfort and defensiveness when confronted about injustice in the land displayed through his and others' attitudes, actions, inaction, and silence. They see the justice scales are not balanced. Justice's eyes are not blinded.

Fear won't keep them from speaking up when they know justice's truth. They see injustice's realities are uncovered as the emperor and his helpers keep strutting.

I nevertheless see them with hope, striving to be justice pursuers until they bring justice to victory (Matthew 12:20).

This is what justice looks like to me.

Rev. Dr. Joseph C. Parker Jr., Esq., who considers himself a pursuer of justice, is an attorney and senior pastor of the David Chapel Missionary Baptist Church in Austin. He has served David Chapel as a minister since 1982 and as senior pastor since 1992.

20

Justice looks like knowing your neighbor

Jorge Zayasbazan

Justice looks like the Great Commandment, "Love the Lord your God with all your heart and with all your soul and with all your strength and with all your mind and, love your neighbor as yourself" (Matthew 22:37–38; Mark 12:30–31; Luke 10:27).

In Matthew, Jesus added that the Law and the demands of the prophets are based on this.

It's that simple, but we want to complicate things. Like the lawyer in Luke 10, we ask, "Who is my neighbor?"

Laws, amendments to the US Constitution, and progressive codes of ethics have failed to eradicate injustice, disparity, and brutality. More of the same will not yield better results.

The problem is in the human heart. We prefer to hang around people who look like us, act like us or, at least, agree with our point of view. This is exacerbated when we unfriend people on social media with whom we disagree and is accelerated by today's cancel culture. We not only hate our enemies but also the friends of our enemies.

Like and unlike

Our desire to exclude those unlike us leads to injustice. We created deed restrictions to keep undesirable people groups out of our neighborhoods. By the time such restrictions were outlawed by the Civil Rights Act of 1968, the damage was done.

Poor, unrestricted neighborhoods were considered high risk and denied mortgage loans—a process known as redlining. Greenlined were the new houses in the suburbs, and everyone who could left the deteriorating cities for better schools and safer neighborhoods—a process known as white flight.

While America officially desegregated schools, lunch counters, and jobs, people continued to self-segregate in social settings. Martin Luther King Jr. repeatedly declared, "Eleven o'clock Sunday morning is the most segregated hour in America."

Racial injustice is fueled by unfamiliarity. An August 2014 article in the *Atlantic* reported that 75 percent of white Americans have entirely white social networks.[1] On the other hand, 65 percent of Black Americans have entirely Black social networks.

As a result, our understanding of people who are different from us comes from stereotypes, caricatures, and media coverage that supports our prejudice.

Jesus is our example

We need to follow Jesus' example. He was called a friend of tax collectors and sinners. He lifted the standing of women and Samaritans. He was not afraid to touch lepers. His followers would open the kingdom of God to non-Jews and a sexually altered Ethiopian.

We must move beyond protests, advocacy, and sensitivity training. Like the "good" Samaritan, we must reach across to people who are different from us with acts of healing and love.

Amy Cooper, the "Central Park Karen," illustrates how far we are from a just society.[2] She was a professional in the finance industry and received the types of racial sensitivity training common in today's corporate environment. In fact, when she called 911 to report a false threat, she used the politically correct term "African American."

She knew a call from a white woman reporting an attack by a Black male will receive immediate attention that could cost the Black male his life. Regardless of her level of racism, she did not see this man as a neighbor deserving of her love.

In the aftermath, they took her dog, fired her from her job, filed criminal charges, and vilified her in the media. These actions

[1] https://www.theatlantic.com/national/archive/2014/08/self-segregation-why-its-hard-for-whites-to-understand-ferguson/378928/.

[2] https://www.foxnews.com/us/birdwatcher-central-park-karen-refuses-to-cooperate.

visibly demonstrate our collective outrage, but we cannot neglect to look within our own hearts. Amy Cooper's act demonstrates the evil that lurks within, ready to spring into action when triggered by the right set of circumstances.

Addressing sin

The underlying problem is sin, and the only solution is Jesus. Racial bias and all types of inequality demonstrate an absence of love for our neighbor. It is an issue Christians of all races, from the entire socioeconomic spectrum, must address together.

First, we must have fellowship. We must share meals. We must work together on projects of mutual interest.

Then, we talk about deeper issues as friends, as true brothers and sisters in Christ.

We need not ever ask, "Who is my neighbor?"

Rev. Jorge Zayasbazan is the pastor of Baptist Temple in San Antonio.

21

Justice looks like living in the light of justification

Kimlyn J. Bender

First and foremost for Christians, justice is seen in light of God's justification of sinners.

The cross is the demonstration of God's righteousness and the pronouncement of God's condemnation upon all human sin and injustice in human history (Romans 3:21–26; 8:1–4). Yet even as all stand under the judgment of the cross because "all have sinned" (Romans 3:23), so all stand under the cross' single mercy.

That God's final word was not to give us the wages of what we deserve but to save us by the gift of his grace in Christ should drive Christians in gratitude to embrace mercy and seek justice. This fact disallows moral hubris and self-righteousness without diminishing the seriousness with which God takes sin.

For those who follow Christ, justice, mercy, and humility must be bound together as a threefold cord (Micah 6:8). Kindness without justice is sentimentality, as justice without kindness is vengeance.

From these convictions, Christians are propelled to strive for justice and oppose injustice in the present beyond the boundaries of the church.

Christian convictions about justice

Creation and God's image

Because all people are created in the image of God—which is the image of Christ—Christians will uphold and lend their aid to elements in the cultural, societal, and political order that uphold the dignity of all people—and do so with special compassion for the vulnerable.

Christians will uphold justice for those who are wronged without depriving those punished for wrongdoing of their own humanity, praying and working for their eventual spiritual and societal restoration.

Sin and salvation

Because all people are caught up in and willingly embrace the powers of sin, Christians will defer to God absolute judgments upon persons, focusing instead on provisional judgments and on the actions and injustices of individuals.

The witness of David's and Paul's lives in Scripture teaches us persons can be both the perpetrators and the victims of injustice. Persons are captive to forces and powers larger than themselves while also possessing the dignity of responsible agency before God—a precondition for justice (Deuteronomy 10:17–19; cf. Leviticus 19:15).

The tragedy of this current state is not the last word. God has not abandoned the world to its own dissolution (Romans 8:18–39). Christians, therefore, can work for justice without either naïve optimism or unyielding cynicism about the human condition or the possibilities of social arrangements.

Reconciliation

Christians embrace justice—a mark of peace and harmony—because they embrace its true goal of reconciliation, for we are the objects of divine reconciliation and called to its ministry (2 Corinthians 5:18; Colossians 1:20).

For Christians, the peace we have with God is the basis for the peace we have with one another within the church and the reason we can pray and work for peace and justice in our world. This peace in the church is the gift of God, not the achievement of humanity, for he alone has broken down the walls of division through the cross (Ephesians 2:15–16; Galatians 3:28).

The final peace to come will be his gift as well, where "righteousness is at home" (2 Peter 3:13).

Final justice and future hope

Christians know final justice is established by God alone and awaits a future hope. This strange time between Christ's resurrection and return is marred by perpetual conflict. Justice in this context is debated perennially not only because of human limitations of knowledge but because any current society is not the kingdom of God and never will be.

Despite having their eyes on a prize beyond this world (Hebrews 11:1), Christians should not be passive but should be faithfully obedient to God in the present order. It is not in spite of but because of Christians' being heavenly minded that they are of earthly good.

The prison reforms of Gladys Aylward in China; the love and care for thousands of orphans in England by George Müller; the protection and compassion given to Jews by Corrie ten Boom and her family during the Second World War; the striving for the abolition of slavery by individuals like Sojourner Truth, William Wilberforce, and Olaudah Equiano—all of these were efforts for justice and opposition to injustice by people driven by faith in a coming kingdom, a faith that did not stifle but propelled their work in our own present world.

The vision of the peaceful kingdom of the future drove Christians to pray and labor for justice and peace in the present and to keep their eyes on a heavenly prize making an earthly one possible. It motivated Christians in ancient Rome to collect and raise unwanted infants—most often girls—abandoned to die on the hills surrounding the city. It also upheld those who marched in Selma for the recognition of the human dignity of all US citizens and the extension of full civil rights and enfranchisement regardless of skin color.

Perseverance in doing good

Christians are called to pray for God's perfect justice to come even as they work to struggle for it now and to embrace all that might reflect it. That they can do so tirelessly is possible only because they do not place their hope in the effervescent whims of human interest, the simplistic optimism of cultural progress, the narrow belief that politics is the only significant lever of human change, or even their own fervent activity.

Instead, Christians place their hope in and wait upon the Lord, the one who renews their strength for calm, resolute, and clear-eyed action within the church and within the world. He allows them to run and not grow weary in doing good while they await their future hope. Theirs is a "hastening that waits."

Kimlyn J. Bender is professor of Christian theology at Baylor University's Truett Theological Seminary. An ordained Baptist minister, he is the author of a number of books, including Reading Karl Barth for the Church: A Guide and Companion *and* 1 Corinthians *in the Brazos Theological Commentary on the Bible series. He is the recipient of numerous awards, including the Elie Wiesel Prize in Ethics.*

22

Justice looks like an America that can celebrate its diversity

Rev. Dr. Michael Evans Sr.

Not since September 11, 2001, has there been a more tumultuous year of the twenty-first century than the year 2020. Please consider the facts.

Sources of tumult in 2020

Our country has struggled with a global pandemic that has claimed, as of this writing, the lives of more than three hundred thousand people and counting. This once-in-a-century event has caused the restriction of religious gatherings, halted sporting events, closed school systems, and placed a pause on life as we know it.

The pandemic, in turn, has plunged the country into a deep recession that has resulted in the loss of millions of jobs. In addition to the public health mayhem, the citizens of our country were made to witness and even experience the anguish and rage that has been a lingering cancer and disease in the Black and Brown communities in America for more than a century.

Millions of people witnessed on national television the death of George Floyd, one more person of color who died while in police custody. George Floyd was not a celebrity of note. He tragically was one of many African American males who lost his life during an arrest attempt in a metropolitan city in our country.

As a result of George Floyd's death, there have been demonstrations in small towns and in metropolitan areas nationwide; in many cases the demonstrations and protests persist. Just like spectators at a theatrical performance, we have witnessed the outpouring of emotions by thousands of people of all ethnicities, skin colors, socioeconomic classes, and levels of education.

The outcry of the masses has resounded in unison, saying that the disproportionate killing and harassment of Black and Brown people groups must stop.

Still do not understand

While the events of the present day are shocking and appalling to many, I discovered a long time ago that many of my well-meaning friends and colleagues still do not understand the gravity of the situation:

- They do not understand that systemic racism continues to pervade our country today.
- They do not understand the disproportionate differences in criminal sentences for offenders of one race versus another.
- They do not understand, or maybe cannot understand, the pain of prejudice and bigotry.
- They do not understand that the phrase "Black Lives Matter" is more descriptive and personal than a political action group.
- They do not understand that the tears so many Black people cry emanate from a place deep within the souls of a people who must (1) assimilate in order to be accepted; (2) whose male role models often are softened in the media and, in order to be tolerated or recognized, are forced to be seen as effeminate; and (3) who fear their child's first traffic stop may be his/her last traffic stop.

Many really don't understand our journey. Lost on so many are the words of James Weldon Johnson:

Stony the road we trod,
bitter the chast'ning rod,
felt in the day that hope unborn had died;
yet with a steady beat,
have not our weary feet,

come to the place on which our fathers sighed?
We have come over a way that with tears has been watered,
we have come, treading our path through the blood of the
 slaughtered,
out from the gloomy past, till now we stand at last
where the white gleam of our star is cast.[1]

What justice looks like to me

Justice looks like an America that can celebrate its diversity. It is a place where character counts instead of the color or pigmentation of one's skin. It is the full recognition that, as human beings, we are created in the "image of God" and are brothers and sisters coequal and composing the human race.

Not until we see the utter humanity and commonalities that exist in all of us can we truly grasp the worth of all people.

As Christians, the lessons of loving one's neighbor in the same manner in which one is to love him or herself should be easy. Unfortunately, we tend to be the people who seemingly are awe-stricken and confused by the outcry of people who have lived with systemic inequities.

Jesus makes it clear; he prioritized the worth of all people when he said, "Truly, I say to you, as you did it to one of the least of these my brothers, you did it to me" (Matthew 25:40).

In the words of an unknown author, "We shall know the true meaning of justice when we come to realize that an injury to one is the concern of us all."

Rev. Dr. Michael Evans Sr. is the pastor of Bethlehem Baptist Church in Mansfield, Texas, and a past president of the Baptist General Convention of Texas. In December 2020, Evans was elected the first Black mayor of Mansfield.

---

[1]   https://www.poetryfoundation.org/poems/46549/lift-every-voice-and-sing.

23

Justice requires having eyes that see

Suzii Paynter March

What does justice look like? The first step of justice is sharpening our ability to see.

Jesus' own miracles so often involved healing the blind. In these acts, Jesus repeatedly reminds all of us we have a blind spot, and God's justice requires two kinds of seeing—eyes of conviction and eyes of compassion.

God gave me eyes of conviction when I heard the plaintive cry of a six-year-old Black child screaming over and over, "Nothing's wrong! Nothing's wrong!"

He saw an X on a paper, and in total frustration, he looked up at the teacher and screamed, "Nothing's wrong!"

He was right. The X was the letter in the word "fox," but he thought the X on his paper meant his work was all wrong.

"Nothing's wrong," he screamed, with tears about to fall.

He woke me up to the experience of children who have been told they are wrong so often by age six that they know the letter X means, "*You* are bad" even if they don't know it is a benign letter in the word "fox."

Seeing in a moment

Eyes of conviction turn inward at a moment of insight, that moment when you realize something was there all along, but you didn't see it. Your expectations, your assumptions, your privilege, your need, your sin—it all kept you from seeing . . . until one moment of revelation.

Some people say, "Now, I'm woke." Others say, "I never knew that before. So that is what it feels like to be told you are bad over and over. That's what it feels like to be on the receiving end of prejudice."

Justice is a place where understanding meets action. Justice looks like waking up. Justice looks like seeing. Justice looks like admitting you were behind the curve and need to catch up. Justice means marshalling my personal power—whatever that is—and putting that power shoulder to the wheel for the sake of a common and bigger good.

Seeing with compassionate wholeness

Justice looks like compassion, not the greeting card version, but the place where I will relinquish the passionate concern I carry around for myself and my self-preservation and trade it in for sheer joy in someone else's delight.

I think of Jesus stopping mid-step in a bustling crowd and saying, "Someone touched me," and then turning amid the business of the day to the outstretched hand of a bleeding woman crawling along in shame.

"You are healed," he said.

"You are healed" was his compassion. It was her delight, and it was an example of God's justice.

Jesus restored God-given health, putting her body in order. Justice is making people whole, making lives whole, restoring human qualities of dignity, opportunity, flourishing, joy.

Seeing the many forms of justice

Justice is the keys to a Habitat house in a strong hand. Justice is decent legal representation or a competent court-appointed special advocate.

Justice is a second chance. Justice is time spent with someone else's problems and someone else's pain. Justice is sometimes eked out over a thorny path of details.

One hot night, I felt justice after eighteen hours of wrangling with the payday lender to free a night nurse from predatory debt.

Her words were "thank you." Her experience and mine were rescuing justice from the jaws of a predator.

Justice and righteousness, conviction, compassion—justice looks like something from God because when you are done, you are depleted, and you also are restored.

Suzii Paynter March was at the time of this writing CEO of Prosper Waco, a nonprofit addressing education, health, and financial security from a perspective of addressing equity issues. March is also a former director of the Texas Baptist Christian Life Commission and executive coordinator of the Cooperative Baptist Fellowship.

24

Justice requires a biblical—stable—foundation
Ricardo Brambila

Justice is a child looking toward a horizon of open opportunities and various paths to reach his or her God-given purpose. Justice is a child who knows they are growing in an environment where his or her best interest is essential to caregivers. Justice is a child who can be accepted and loved for who he or she is. Justice is a child who can love himself or herself just as he or she was made in the image of God.

Looking at justice as a child

When I hear *justice* as a first-generation Hispanic who has lived in the United States since age thirteen, my thinking is shaped by growing up in a border town.

These impoverished border communities know of justice as something only wealthy people can obtain. Justice is a commodity with a price. Corruption and justice are tied together for the benefit of those in a position of power and authority.

In this environment of injustice, you soon learn to survive and navigate through these systems. These systems are set to ensure that as you grow, you know your place; you know your limitations and what is meant to be for you.

For example, there are sectors, or *colonias*, of housing where you are marginalized. Schools and people will ask, "Where do you live?" Your home address will tell a story of your socioeconomic status and ethnic origin.

Growing up in a border town, you knew the solution to reach justice was to walk and cross the Rio Grande just two miles north to the land where you can begin the pursuit of happiness. Growing up on the border, you knew the country you were born in would be an essential piece of your life to find purpose, justice, and hope.

Seeking justice as a youth

In my experience, coming to the United States in my teen years, I felt, finally, justice was attainable regardless of my socioeconomic status and ethnic origin.

It is imperative to understand that, when you come from poverty, any opportunity is a stepping-stone to achieve purpose, justice, and hope. To understand this last sentence, you must see it from the perspective of living where there is no hope and no justice; from there, any hope and opportunity is better than no hope and no justice.

I soon realized that, while there was more justice, hope, and opportunity, there is a past in this country of injustice against African Americans and immigrant minorities. As an immigrant, you soon realize there is a limited expectation of who and what an immigrant represents.

While many can reach legal immigrant status, the profiling of your ethnic origin will be with you as a shadow.

Important questions

How do we find justice, and how do we create an environment of justice?

Justice, according to the Scriptures and in its Hebrew context, has three main roots: (1) to punish what is not just, (2) to make straight anything that is not according to standard, and (3) to act according to the moral standard by which God measures human conduct.

According to Romans 2:13, it is not the hearers of the law who are just in God's sight, but the doers of the law.

There is justice that comes from our Lord and King, and there is a justice expected from our Lord and King.

If a person finds justice, such a person has found purpose and meaning for his or her life. Justice is what took Jesus to the cross, and justice is what was given to each person who believes. He made straight what was twisted. He redeemed the believer with justice.

I believe creating an environment of justice begins with each person considering one's ways in light of the moral standard of the word of God.

Some important questions are, How can we claim justice if we are in spiritual bankruptcy? How can we claim justice if we keep rejecting the biblical standard?

To make anything right, there must be a standard base. If we reject any biblical moral standard, then what is the standard?

Without a biblical foundation, the standard becomes like that in the time of the judges. "In those days there was no king in Israel; everyone did what was right in his own eyes" (Judges 17:6; 21:25 NKJV).

Ricardo Brambila is the pastor of Primera Iglesia Bautista Dallas and the executive director of the West Dallas Community School. He was the director for Buckner Family Hope Center in Bachman Lake. He grew up in the Rio Grande Valley and now resides in Dallas. He has been married for seventeen years to Janeth Brambila, and they have three children.

25

Justice looks like anti-racism

Jon Singletary

The white church in America is learning racism is not merely about our individual actions and decisions.

As civil human beings—more so as children of God—we know better than to be racist, than to do racist things. In fact, in our effort not to be racists, we work hard to talk as though race doesn't exist. Being colorblind was the way to be non-racist, we were taught. I suppose it meant if we didn't see race, we couldn't perpetuate it or contribute to racism.

Beverly Daniel Tatum introduced us to the idea that being non-racist is not the end goal for racial justice. Even if my actions and decisions are wholesome, faithful, and just, I am part of a world in which racism affects the Black people in my life. Racism is in our schools, our nonprofits, and our churches—even the best ones, even the ones seeking racial justice.

Racism is about systems

Racism, therefore, is not simply about my actions; it is about systems that are predominantly white, that have not embraced Blackness, and, as a result, remain oppressive, exploitative, and marginalizing.

Nice white people are still complicit in racist structures. And the nice white places we love still hurt Black people. Here, Black voices are on the margins, Black leaders are asked to do more than their fair share to help white people manage race relations, and Black brothers and sisters never experience our ideal when white family members make the decisions and call the shots.

Anti-racism is required

As a result, anti-racism is what is required of us, and it requires more from us than being non-racist. Anti-racism requires working actively against the racism of our structures in a society where the white way is the right way, even when unintentional.

Anti-racism requires a cultural humility to listen to and learn from the Black community. Doing so will elicit feelings that must move from white guilt to godly grief, as Jemar Tisby teaches. From that grief, we are able to join in lament.

Then, we are able to move to the love of neighbor God asks of us and join in the work of liberation. This liberation is a genuine freedom for Black people from white systems and toward the possibility of mutual, meaningful relationships.

Justice, not reconciliation

These efforts are not about racial reconciliation—which is a myth, since Black and white Americans never have had a relationship that can be reconciled—but about racial justice.

Racial justice is work for fair treatment and equal outcomes for Black people and people of all races. Racial justice is a reflection of God's desire that all people be treated with dignity and respect. Racial justice is the recognition we all bear God's image and likeness with equal status.

The essence of God is within each Black child of God, and we therefore must highlight how Black lives not only matter but are essential to life together in Christ. It is easy to say, but it requires work.

The good news of the gospel of Christ for all people requires nothing less of us than this work of anti-racism for racial justice. The work of God within us calls us to see God in others. Through cultural humility, we can see other people as the experts of their experiences.

The work of God within us calls us to see the racism still present all around us. Ignoring this keeps us culpable in perpetuating racism; our silence is violence.

And the work of God within us calls us to see anti-racism is the journey toward the kingdom goal of racial justice.

Jon Singletary is the dean of Baylor University's Diana R. Garland School of Social Work.

26

Justice looks like a healthy relationship

Kirk Stowers

Seemingly competing demands to defund the police and to promote law and order agree on the same goal—to have justice.

Justice can be in the form of strict enforcement of rules, adjusting policy relating to demographic outcomes, providing equal distribution of resources, or mitigating harm done to a person. Perhaps viewing justice like a healthy relationship can lead to accomplishing each of these forms.

Justice requires discerning intent

There are times when an on-duty and uniformed police officer goes to the register to pay for a meal at a restaurant only to be told the person ahead of the officer already paid for the meal.

There are times when a person lowers his or her window at the stoplight to get the attention of an officer in his patrol car just to express gratitude and appreciation for the service he provides to the community.

There are teachers who deliver notes from students communicating admiration and praise for police service.

Police officers are trained to reject anything of value or benefit because those things may be attempts at bribery. In fact, police are trained to look for criminal intent and to protect themselves from the bad acts of bad actors.

The normal case study involves something bad that happened to a police officer leading officers after that event to protect themselves by preparing and positioning themselves to avoid the possibility of that bad thing happening to them. Police officers even watch videos of these events.

Just as often, experienced officers coach new officers that not everyone is out to get them.

Types of officers

David Wood, who spent time in prison, explains why some people hate cops in a video posted to YouTube in connection with his ministry, Acts 17 Apologetics.[1]

Speaking about prison guards, Wood describes five types of officers:

- one who shows up merely to collect a paycheck;
- one who is relaxed on enforcement in order to be popular;
- one who genuinely believes the offender made a mistake and works to solve problems and extends grace;
- one who wants to modify others' behavior through swift, certain consequences;
- and one who genuinely is corrupt.

Wood says the corrupt officer is the only one remembered among all other encounters with police. He also says trying to resolve problems with a corrupt officer's conduct can be frustrated by systems that appear to protect the corrupt officer.

Good and bad cops

The officers Wood describes are people who can be found in any occupation. One truth to be noted is good cops hate bad cops, and the good want to get rid of the bad as quickly as possible and often do.

The action to get rid of bad conduct is more aggressive in law enforcement than in any other place of employment of which I am aware. Police officers commonly are more worried about what

---

[1]   The video referenced was accessed at https://www.youtube.com/watch?v=TnD5lS-rHJY and has subsequently been removed from YouTube by its creator, David Wood, who explains this decision in a separate video on Apologetics 315: https://apologetics315.com/videos/acts-17-apologetics/?wchannelid=7gugggjeoo&wmediaid=szm7z8whdd.

actions administrators take against them than what someone in the public might do to them during a service call.

Seeking justice in law enforcement

The effort to seek justice requires dialogue and action. To resolve conflicts, we often must give up something to build a bridge of compromise.

To manage people we love, we often have to forgive and extend grace. Like the father in the parable of the prodigal son in Luke 15:11–32, we should value the people even when they have wronged us.

Let's stop focusing on how we have been wronged and focus on the good we do to each other. It's a natural trait to be angry and dwell on the bad, but it is godly and more constructive to extend grace within meaningful boundaries. When we do that, justice will look like a healthy relationship.

Kirk Stowers holds a master of arts in ministry degree from Stark College and Seminary, is associate pastor of Travis Baptist Church in Corpus Christi, and serves as board president of the Council on Alcohol and Drug Abuse of the Coastal Bend. Stowers has been employed full time in law enforcement since 2002 and presently serves on patrol with a municipal police department serving a population over 350,000.

27

Justice needs you. I need you.

Rev. Dr. Kan'Dace Brock

I am tired, and I need you. Since COVID-19 has ravished life as we knew it, it seems as though the racial and socioeconomic plight of Black and brown communities has been placed front and center. Not because we've done it, but because COVID-19 has shown it does not care which box one checks on the 2020 census.

Sad to say, COVID-19 isn't the first pandemic Black and brown communities have been fighting. Black and brown people have been fighting racism more than four hundred years. For more than four hundred years, Black and brown people have struggled to have their humanity seen. When it is seen, it is usually seen in a negative, twisted light.

For years, Blacks have fought for a piece of the American Dream only to be told we will never obtain this alleged dream because our hair is too coarse and our skin has been kissed by the sun.

From the first day I could remember, my parents had to raise me to understand I am a Black child who will grow up to be a Black woman in a world that may or may not accept me. Can you imagine having to grow up with the weight of your people resting on your shoulders?

My parents would go on to say, "If you are accepted, make sure you open the door for others. And if you aren't accepted, continue to lean into your faith because it is in your faith you will learn how to cope with being Black in America."

Did I mention, I am tired?

Why I am tired

I am tired of those who co-opt Black culture but refuse to speak up for #Blacklivesmatter because the sanitized version is #Alllivesmatter.

I am tired of being seen but not heard.

I am tired of having to fear for the life of my husband and daughter.

I am tired of fearing for the life of my father, my father-in-law, my brother-in-law, my uncles, cousins, nephews, neighbors, and parishioners.

I am tired of seeing the hashtags and t-shirts of a life cut short at the hands of reckless law enforcement.

I am tired of being the token Black woman so a company can check off their list the box for diversity and inclusion.

I am tired of being followed in a store because someone of ivory hue believes I am there to steal.

I am tired of my credentials being scrutinized and the perception of my people and me dramatized.

I am tired of wondering, "Will I be next?"

Did I mention I am tired?

How I need you

I could go on and on about my racial fatigue, but I will refrain. Instead, I will tell you I need you.

I need you to facilitate race-related conversations within your circles of influence.

I need you to ask questions and expect answers.

I need you to ask your congregations, denominational leaders, and others to pray and also to pair actions with their prayers.

I need you to ask why there aren't any Black or brown bodies in the room.

I need you to ask yourself, "When was the last time I read or cited the work of a Black or Hispanic theologian or author?"

I need you to ask yourself, "When was the last time I celebrated Black History Month or National Hispanic Heritage Month?"

I need you to address the racism within your circle and ask yourself, "Why do I feel this way? Where did these feelings of hatred come from? Why am I insensitive to the plight of others? Why do I have malice in my heart?"

And I need you to ask the ultimate question, "Why am I so afraid?"

I need you to have these conversations. After all, I and many others will never be afforded this conversation because I am "too emotional."

I need you more than ever. I need your voice. I need your persuasion. I need your influence. But most of all, I need you.

As you seek God in what you should do, I ask you to remember my eternal fatigue and your brothers and sisters of ebony hue.

Above all, I ask you to remember the humanity of all people, not just some.

Rev. Dr. Kan'Dace Brock, LMSW, is the lead pastor of The Message Church in San Antonio.

28

Learning justice demands all of me

Gaynor Yancey

"The LORD works righteousness and justice for all the oppressed" (Psalm 103:6 NIV).

"God makes everything come out right; he puts victims back on their feet" (*The Message*, Psalm 103:6).

Christian Scriptures give great hope for the oppressed and victims of oppression. No matter which translation of the Bible we read, it is clear in Psalm 103:6 that God knows about the oppression and the resulting victimization.

The Bible is full of admonitions to followers of the way of Jesus about our actions toward the oppressed and victimized. We are to treat all people with love, dignity, honor, and justice because we all are made in the image of God.

Our actions should flow naturally from a heart filled with God's love. Learning to see people as God would have us see them, with loving actions toward and on behalf of all people, comes with a commitment to do this hard work with the Lord. That commitment, I have discovered, is a life-long journey.

Learning about justice as a child

As a child, I never heard about justice. In church, we studied about social issues, but justice was not a concept ever taught to me then.

During my elementary school years, I grew up in Pittsburgh, Pennsylvania. Over the July 4 holiday week, my father's company always would close, and we would drive to Patmos, Arkansas, to visit my father's family, who were farmers in this rural area outside of Hope, Arkansas.

One summer, as we drove through Mississippi, we stopped to get gas and for my brother and me to run around the grassy area by the gas station. I was thirsty and went to the water fountain to get a drink of water. As I got to that public water fountain, a little boy who was Black came up to me and said I could not drink from this water fountain because it was only for people who were Black.

I thought I had done something terribly wrong, but my father told me he wanted me to understand it was not right, that the water was the same, and that the little boy could drink from the water fountain designated for people who were white, and I could drink from the water fountain designated for people who were Black. There was absolutely no difference in the water, and it was for everyone.

I remember saying to my father it was not fair if the little boy or I got in trouble for drinking from those water fountains. That occasion was my first experience with justice and injustice.

Learning about justice as a teenager

Then in high school, two different events occurred. One of our church friends got pregnant and was not married. In church, we were taught not to have anything to do with people who had "sin" in their lives. If we did, their sin would rub off on us. So, sadly, instead of surrounding this teen friend with our support and love, we basically left her alone.

At the same time, we had a member of our girls' basketball team develop a crush on one of the other girls. No one knew she was gay, and, again, we basically left her alone.

In these examples, we were acting in ways we understood Christians should act. We were so very wrong. We definitely were not treating both of these girls with honor and dignity, nor were we showing them any type of Christian love. These were experiences where justice should have been practiced. These were my first experiences with what I now sadly refer to as a gospel of exclusion.

Studying justice in all of life and the Bible

My high school and college years were spent in the turbulence of the 1960s, with racial unrest, assassinations of our leaders, free-flowing drugs, disrespect for authority and for the US flag, and so much more.

Cities being burned and people protesting for just employment practices, better housing, better education, and more opportunities were a part of daily life. It was during those days that justice became something I began to study.

Our inhumanity toward each other was profound. As I studied and observed our human behaviors toward each other, I began to understand *everything* we read in the Bible is aimed at focusing on treating each other with the deep love God has for all of us as God's children.

It was then I began to understand it is most important we learn how to walk alongside each other without labeling people while being supportive, encouraging, and loving in the ways God asks of us. I was starting to understand what justice meant in a relational way through the examples Jesus gave us.

Learning just what justice demands of me

Our actions show what is in our hearts. When I first went to Philadelphia as a career missionary, I had no idea what it was like to be as economically poor as this community was. I had no idea what it was like to be kicked out of the church because I was not married and had multiple children. I had no idea what it was like to be sexually exploited. I had no idea what it was like.

What I did understand was that all my life I thought I was sharing with others about God's love. What I came to understand was I was sharing God's love with only those people who were just like me. Through the patience of those marginalized in multiple ways, I learned the gospel truly is about inclusion, not exclusion.

What God wanted me to do was to be working with all people, with no qualifiers. That was a major revelation in my life.

The Scriptures tell us the parable of putting new wine into old wineskins (Mark 2:22). God needed my heart to be emptied of the old stuff before he could fill my heart with the newness of God's ways I now understood and that I am continuing to understand.

Only through that lengthy experience was I ready to do what God called me to do in loving people and working for justice. Justice demands all of me.

Gaynor Yancey is a professor in Baylor University's Diana R. Garland School of Social Work and Truett Seminary and the director of the Center for Church and Community Impact. She is the holder of the Lake Family Foundation Endowed Chair in Congregational and Community Health.

29

Justice is the right key to the right door

Rev. Cokiesha Bailey Robinson

A friend recently asked me, "How can we, as your white brothers and sisters, promote racial reconciliation in these hard times and beyond?" I appreciated the question.

I believe my answer, in short, is justice, diversity, equity, and inclusion.

Justice, diversity, equity, and inclusion look like arrows to me that point us to racial reconciliation. Racial reconciliation is a gift birthed from justice.

A benefit of that would be a world with a greater commitment to rejecting racist cultures and to promoting of anti-racist cultures.

Right now, people are "punch drunk," as they say in the boxing world, from the hard blows of the health, economic, and racial pandemics.

Some are clueless or insensitive because they have not been directly impacted by the loss of friends or family, loss of jobs, loss of safety, loss of life, or loss of income. We are continuing to watch two Americas at war at the same time.

Time to face racism

The time has come to discuss racism and not to run from the necessary tension. It's uncomfortable, messy work, but necessary work, Christ-inspired work, redemptive work.

A work that should require a lifetime commitment, and one that should force each of us to "die daily" (1 Corinthians 15:21).

We must take a look at racism—the original sin of America—and its consequences.

We must sit in grief with one another, hear one another, and find solutions that don't dilute the pain of the past but encourage a culturally competent future.

We must look at who we hire and how many faces and backgrounds that look the same and how many that look different are welcomed. We must ask ourselves, "Are underrepresented people valued and welcomed, and do we see 'the proof in the pudding' on our rosters, websites, org charts, images we promote, and on our payroll?"

We must hire all people and have processes and policies that ensure it.

We must be open to dialogue about what diversity, equality, and inclusion mean and what justice looks like to others.

We must also be careful not to skate around conversations on social justice in the gospel, in the church, in relationships, in the workplace, and in the community.

A seat and a voice

Many want racial reconciliation divorced from social justice. It's not possible, and neither is it biblical.

"He has told you, O man, what is good; and what does the Lord require of you but to do justice, and to love kindness, and to walk humbly with your God?" (Micah 6:8).

Justice must be wrapped up in humility, repentance, lamentation, forgiveness, shared experiences, shared opportunities, equity, and reconciliation.

Justice is not one-sided. It includes all people at the table with equal and distributed power.

One writer said, "Diversity is having a seat at the table; inclusion is having a voice at the table; and belonging is having that voice be heard."

To me justice, diversity, and inclusion provide a table, a seat, a voice, and an opportunity that promotes reconciliation.

A question toward justice

What are practical ways we can impact change right now by being just?

By inviting minority leaders to the table. Are women at your table? Are Asian, African, Indian, and Islander leaders at your table? Are leaders with disabilities at your table? Are African American and Latinx male and female leaders at your table on every level? Are there people at your table who do not share your political, social, or theological views?

When the answer is "Yes," that's when justice is in view.

It is not a moment. It is a movement. It's not a sprint. It's a marathon.

Dr. Martin Luther King Jr. said, "We must forever continue our struggle on the high plane of dignity and discipline."

Dignity and discipline—those are the keys to the future that open the doors of justice to me.

May we not be at the right place with the wrong key.

Rev. Cokiesha Bailey Robinson is the associate dean of student diversity and inclusion at Grace College and Seminary in Winona Lake, Indiana.

30

Justice must precede peace, calm, and healing

Jeremy K. Everett

In the days and weeks after a tumultuous transfer of US presidential administrations, pastors and public servants around the country asked themselves, "How do we calm the ideological storm raging in America?"

What sermons can we preach or speeches can we give to heal a divided country, divided communities, and divided congregations?

I even have heard commentators from conservative media outlets wonder, with a hopeful tone, "Can President Biden bring healing to this hurting nation?"

Admittedly, I also want peace. I want calm. I want healing. I want government and even church to be boring again. But peace, calm, and healing cannot precede justice.

If we attempt to skip the Christ-inspired work of caring for the impoverished, providing food for the hungry, ensuring health care for the sick and justice for our brothers and sisters of color, we are not simply divided; we are delusional. That is not how the equations of peace and justice work.

No justice, no peace.

Since the beginning of the pandemic, rates of food insecurity in the United States have doubled.

My colleague Elaine Waxman, senior fellow at the Urban Institute, found while the initial round of pandemic relief improved the situation somewhat for people who had lost their incomes, "by fall 2020, more than 1 in 5 adults were living in food insecure households, about the same proportion as in the early weeks of the pandemic."[1]

Sadly, but predictably, these hardships weren't spread evenly among all Americans. Waxman and her team found food insecurity rates among Black and Hispanic/Latinx adults were roughly double that of white adults.

We also know from research that those experiencing food insecurity are among the most at risk for COVID-19, job loss, and underemployment. They are bearing the weight of our broken social systems in the United States.

The church's part in justice

What role can congregations play when the challenge is so daunting?

One of the primary answers to this question is faith formation. Transforming any of the challenges amplified in recent months—from food insecurity, health inequities made increasingly visible during the pandemic, to structural racism—we need to make straight theologically crooked paths that allow our congregations to remain silent or indifferent to injustice.

We need to come to terms with the uncomfortable truth. Many of our congregations and denominations provide a theological framework that allows these injustices to occur. This will require us courageously to set aside worries about how our message of repentance will be received and simply preach it.

The biblical witness is clear. Injustice is sin. If people do not have enough food in a world that produces more than enough food for everyone, an injustice is present.

Structural injustice is structural sin. If particular populations bear the weight of poverty and hunger more than others, then that is a structural injustice. Any of us who have spent more than a few minutes in a Baptist Sunday school class know the answer to sin is repentance.

---

[1] https://www.urban.org/research/publication/food-insecurity-edged-back-after-covid-19-relief-expired.

Walk with those who suffer

This Sunday, when we pray, "Give us this day our daily bread," we pray not only for ourselves and our families but also for those who are hungry.

We commit ourselves to walk alongside those suffering from injustice as an act of solidarity. We commit to walking alongside them in and through their suffering and to working with them to make the crooked paths of injustice straight to end their suffering. This is faith formation informing societal transformation.

Churches do not have to walk this path alone. Organizations and individuals in our communities have been dedicated to feeding the hungry and healing the sick for some time. They already have the tools to effect change. But they need our help and partnership.

Churches can provide volunteers and resources. They can grow fresh produce on their properties to assist these organizations in bending the world toward justice. In turn, the justice community can educate and inform congregations on how to put their faith into action.

This is how we bring about justice and make room for peace and ultimately heal as a nation.

Jeremy K. Everett is the executive director of the Baylor University Collaborative on Hunger and Poverty and the author of I Was Hungry: Cultivating Common Ground to End an American Crisis.

31

Justice looks like jumping in the water
Michael Mills

If I jumped, I knew I'd be out of my depth. With toes hanging off the edge of the diving board, my swimming instructor was calling out from down below, "Just jump! You'll be fine. If you jump, I'll buy you a candy bar."

Feeling the tension within me, I hesitated. I knew there was risk. I wasn't a strong swimmer, but I was learning. I wanted to trust my swimming instructor. She believed in me, and she was there to support me. Her voice still rings in my ear, "Come on! Jump in. You'll be alright."

I didn't jump that day.

All my life, I've felt like I've been swimming out of my depth. I get my wits about me the moment after the moment has passed.

In school, it was the last day of class when I finally understood the first day of class. In relationships, I cherish people after they're gone. In work, I find the key to unlocking a passage of Scripture as I close my sermon on that Scripture. In matters of justice, well . . . you can probably guess.

Justice rightly is on everyone's minds these days. Cries for justice unsettle any semblance of peace the privileged have. While we want to believe we live in a just world, we don't. And the often-quoted words of Martin Luther King Jr. remind us of the truth of the matter: "Injustice anywhere is a threat to justice everywhere."

Comparing two thinkers on justice

I've been thinking on the "how" question. How do we go about bringing justice for all?

In his *The Cross and the Lynching Tree*, James H. Cone offers an illuminating comparison between Reinhold Niebuhr and Dr. King. His main focus is on the fact Niebuhr, despite a career's worth of opportunity, did not speak directly of the obvious connection between the cross upon which Jesus unjustly died and the commonplace lynching tree upon which thousands of Black men and women died. But King did.

King courageously spoke truth to power, knowing it likely would cost him his life. The comparison is meant to issue a call to speak up because we only have the one life to get it right.

How each of these men contributed to the betterment of society is also of interest to me. Niebuhr was a pragmatist, believing in an incremental approach to improvement. King was a bit more of an idealist, believing in a prophetic vision of equality founded in God.

It's worth asking: While both made significant contributions to this world, who moved the needle more?

Where I find myself

As I think about what justice means to me and my place in the fight for it, I think of Niebuhr and King. I tend to carry the idealism of King within me and the incrementalism of Niebuhr in my engagement. Honestly, I don't know that is best.

I wonder if my hesitancy to engage the fight for justice fully is because I feel like I am, once again, swimming out of my depth. I'm learning, but I am far from knowing it all. I'm sorting it out, but I don't have it all sorted out yet. I'm stepping into the fight, but I'm keeping one foot out the door.

But here is what I am realizing: lives are at stake.

I hear the voice call out to me, "Come on! Jump in!"

This is not the voice of my swim instructor telling me I will be alright. This is the voice of those who are drowning, and they call to me to jump in. Not to save them, but to fight with them.

I know I'm swimming out of my depth. But is that a good reason not to jump in?

Michael Mills was the pastor of Agape Baptist Church in Fort Worth, Texas, which voted to disband in early 2023. Easter was their last Sunday together.

32

Justice looks like "fighting for the good of everyone"

Cynthia Aulds

Sadly, sometimes it is easier to contemplate what justice doesn't look like than what it does.

As director of an organization fighting to combat human trafficking, there unfortunately are many occasions when we fail to see justice prevail.

- When a young teenager takes her own life because she could no longer bear to live with the atrocities she experienced.
- When we have difficulty getting into some schools or churches because those in charge don't want such a difficult topic discussed from their podiums.
- When a person takes advantage of another because of the other's lack of knowledge, education, or perhaps impoverished situation.
- When an individual chooses the lifestyle of "selling" an individual multiple times a day for their own profit and greed and, more often than not, is never held accountable.
- When companies knowingly use force, fraud, or coercion to traffic individuals for their labor needs.

Every individual at risk of being trafficked deserves the opportunity to have the knowledge, awareness, and education to help prevent him or her from becoming victimized.

Pervasiveness of human trafficking

Our organization combats trafficking—both labor and sex—throughout the state of Texas, and sadly, all these are instances that occur throughout Texas, in multiple towns, cities, and communities on a regular basis.

Regardless of where you live, human trafficking is present, and it's real. Texas consistently ranks among the top states in the country for trafficking.

Recent studies show that in the state of Texas there are an estimated 313,000 victims of human trafficking, 234,000 of whom are victims of labor trafficking, 79,000 of whom are children and youth. From the smallest of cities to the largest towns, no one is immune.

Maybe some are runaways. It shouldn't matter.

Maybe some are members of the LGBTQ+ community. It shouldn't matter.

Maybe some are white, Black, Hispanic, or a member of another race. It shouldn't matter.

Maybe some are impoverished. It shouldn't matter.

When people are treated unfairly by others, we must join in a fight for justice on their behalf. If we do all we can to eradicate both sex and labor trafficking and stop the suffering of anyone enmeshed in this horrific industry, then we can say justice has occurred.

What justice means

Justice means we have to have stricter laws. Justice means we have people getting involved with legislation and helping change the laws to hold individuals accountable for their actions and treatment of others.

Justice means we go after those buying the sex and the companies using force, fraud, or coercion to traffic individuals for labor and hold them accountable with stringent penalties.

Justice means we care for all people, regardless of their income level, race, sexual preference, home situations, or any other factors.

Justice means we put our heart and soul into fighting for the good of everyone. God hears the cry of the oppressed, and he certainly wants the wrongs made right. We, as Christians, must engage with one another and love and fight for all.

I had a wise pastor who once said the overriding principle of the Bible is "God is love; love one another."

If we as Christians can live out this edict, justice will prevail for all.

Cynthia Aulds is the director of the Coalition to Combat Human Trafficking in Texas. Before that, she was a missions minister at Sugar Land Baptist Church.

33

Justice looks like God's law

Randy Dale

As if dealing with COVID-19 hasn't been stressful enough, the unfortunate and ill-advised actions of a few police officers once again have ripped the bandage off the ever-seeping wound of racial injustice.

The wound now is gaping open, with pain and blood spilling all over every news outlet and venue in the world. As a result, age-old questions about justice—what it is, what it is not, and what it looks like—have resurfaced at the forefront.

My experience seeking justice

I have been a lawyer for forty-one years, and more than half of that has been as a Texas prosecutor. During that period, I have worked for five different district or county attorneys, having been involved with cases ranging from traffic violations to capital murders.

I have appeared before innumerable judges, gone against innumerable defense attorneys—and was one for a short period—and have worked with a whole host of police officers, state troopers, deputy sheriffs, and officers from a plethora of other agencies.

I even spent two years in Afghanistan mentoring and training judges and prosecutors.

I have been immersed in the sea of justice for more than half of my life. Yet, here we are, asking again, "What is justice?"

That is of no small importance to a prosecutor, as our "duty," per the Texas Code of Criminal Procedure, is not to obtain convictions but to see that "justice is served."

Defining justice

Black's Law Dictionary defines justice as "the constant and perpetual disposition to render every man his due" and "the conformity of our actions and our will to the law."

Clear as Texas crude, right?

Webster offers a clearer framework: "The quality of being just, impartial, or fair."

But, that word, *fair*, also links us to a couple of concepts we, as Christ followers, reflect from him—grace and mercy.

As a seminary student years ago, I learned a good rule of thumb for these two concepts. Grace is giving what is not deserved, and mercy is not giving what is deserved. This brings it home for me.

And speaking of justice and mercy in the same breath, isn't there something in Micah 6 about that?

Justice in the eyes of the law and Law

Where I work, justice means doing the right thing, the right way, the first time, and doing no harm—exonerating the innocent; convicting the guilty with competent, credible evidence; and securing a sentence proportionate and appropriate to the crime, yet tempered with grace and mercy.

Justice is using the law to hold people accountable for hurting others and to restore victims to the position they enjoyed prior to the crime, all the while attempting to perform these duties fairly, consistently, and with no regard whatsoever for the accused's race, gender, age, sexual orientation, economic status, civic position, religion, or profession.

Even police officers are not immune from prosecution for criminal behavior.

I believe the Author and Finisher of our faith expects no less of me.

Randy Dale is Director of Church Engagement for 21 Wilberforce and an adjunct professor of criminal justice at the University of Mary Hardin-Baylor. He is a member of Meadow Oaks Baptist Church in Temple, Texas.

34

Justice looks like a church playground where all can play

Joe Rangel

Thirty-eight years ago, on a Sunday morning, I led a revolt.

My family and I were members of a small Hispanic Baptist mission in North Central Texas. Our mission church held the worship services in the chapel of the "mother church," the Anglo church.

The Hispanic children of the mission had been instructed to play in the toddler play area only. There was a fence that divided the smaller play area from the big playground. On that Sunday morning, I decided to open the gate that divided the playgrounds and invited my friends to join me in the revolt.

My reasoning was simple. It was not fair that we should not be able to play on the big playground. Most of my friends said we should not go to the other side, and yet, I convinced them it would be fine.

Our time of fun on the playground ended abruptly when a church leader from the Anglo church noticed us and came outside to tell us to get off the playground.

I never forgot his words spoken with such anger, "Don't you know you kids belong on the other side of the fence!"

Even as an eight-year-old, as my friends and I ashamedly got off the playground and walked back through the gate, I knew in my heart this was not the way God intended the church playground to be used.

What made us any different than the other kids? Why was it not equitable for the Hispanic children to play on the church's playground like the other children?

The reason for inequity was based on our ethnicity and skin color alone. I knew our painful experience with systemic racism probably hurt God's heart more than it did mine.

For me, justice looks like a church playground with children of all backgrounds and ethnicities playing together equitably, celebrating childhood. I know this probably is not how others would say justice looks, but for me, it does because this image is very personal.

Justice is action

Justice is action, and many times, justice needs to be corrective action against systemic sin that has been ignored or simply tolerated. Justice not only calls out for equality but for equity as well. Equity is the action part of justice that pushes for fairness.

The prophet Micah calls believers to "do" this type of justice, which makes it more than just lip service. Christians no longer can ignore systemic racism. We must engage it and correctively eradicate it, especially when it is in the church.

Growing up, I never forgot that painful memory, and I knew it was wrong based on God's word and his love for all the nations. This event should not have happened on a church playground, and I was set on actively correcting this experience. I needed to do justice.

God led me to pursue a PhD in the School of Intercultural Studies at Biola University. I wanted to learn how to bring cultures and ethnicities together through the gospel and God's church and, yes, even through a playground.

In my studies, I learned what I already knew in my heart. God despises systemic racism and all discriminatory actions. Xenophobia and nationalistic ideology are the prime sinful catalysts for racism and discrimination.

Racist discrimination should never be a part of those "called out" from the former way of thinking and acting to be the church. As the *ekklesia*, we are called out from our sinful patterns to experience a transforming power over our sin nature and to be a community that welcomes all ethnicities in Christ.

Seeing the results of action

Before finishing my doctorate, I was the pastor of a multiethnic church in Southern California. On one particular Sunday morning, as I rushed into the church, God turned my attention to the playground. It was then I saw children of all backgrounds and ethnicities playing together and having fun. It was a great site to see.

What I saw that morning was justice, and any hurt and pain I harbored because of my previous painful experience on a church playground melted away in such a powerful moment.

At Wayland Baptist University, I am the associate dean of the School of Christian Studies, and I teach ministry students biblical truths and methodologies to continue to bring cultures and ethnicities together.

I want my ministry students' future churches and their playgrounds to be places of God's welcoming acceptance. This continues to be my revolt for corrective equitable justice.

Dr. Joe Rangel is the associate dean of the School of Christian Studies and teaches Christian ministry at Wayland Baptist University. He most recently served as executive pastor at First Baptist Church in Weslaco. He is married to Sara, and they have one amazing son.

35

Justice looks like shalom for my neighbor

Anyra Cano

August 2017 was a month I experienced like no other before. I was standing in the Fort Worth City Council meeting, where hundreds of citizens came together to ask the city to join a lawsuit against SB4—a "show me your papers" law passed in Texas.

We did not win the votes necessary. Nonetheless, I saw lived out that day the arduous work of justice for our neighbors.

In that auditorium were people of diverse ethnicities, races, faiths, and socioeconomic backgrounds. The majority were not immigrants, and many had no direct family members who were immigrants. You would think they had no personal motive to be there. The law did not affect them personally since it did not infringe on any of their rights or privileges.

The room was filled with Latinos, African Americans, Jews, Muslims, white people, Catholics, Christians, affluent and vulnerable people, immigrants, students, professors, professionals, and leaders of many fields. All of them were advocating together on behalf of our undocumented immigrant neighbors.

We did so because we wanted our neighbors to be restored, made whole, reconciled, complete. In other words, we wanted them to experience the shalom of God.

I remember one Black neighbor that day who said he stood with the undocumented community because they were his neighbors, and he hoped one day the immigrant community also would stand with and for him.

That day, I witnessed a glimpse of hope for our neighbors.

What shalom looks like

Lisa Sharon Harper says it so well in the summary of her book *The Very Good Gospel: How Everything Wrong Can Be Made Right*:

> Shalom is what God declared. Shalom is what the Kingdom of God looks like. Shalom is when all people have enough. It's when families are healed. It's when churches, schools, and public policies protect human dignity. Shalom is when the image of God is recognized in every single human. Shalom is our calling as followers of Jesus' gospel. It is the vision God set forth in the Garden and the restoration God desires for every relationship.[1]

Shalom is to be made whole. When we see our neighbors are in need, suffering, or facing injustices, we have compassion, and then we act on empathy by seeking the shalom they need to be made complete.

Shalom in Jesus' ministry

As I look to Jesus' ministry, I continually see his desire for shalom in the lives of those who have been oppressed and marginalized, and who are vulnerable.

We have the story of the woman who hemorrhaged for twelve years. Jesus stops to heal her while on his way to heal the daughter of a powerful, influential, and religious man. The daughter dies while Jesus stops to ask who touched him. He offers the woman shalom, restores her health, and reconciles her to her community and himself.

In another story, Jesus goes out of his way to bring wholeness—shalom—to a Samaritan woman who feels abandoned, abused, and insufficient. Jesus offers safety, permanence, and restoration. Then she goes back to the same community that shunned and abused her and extends the good news of Jesus to them, sharing the shalom of Christ with them.

---

[1] Lisa Sharon Harper, *The Very Good Gospel: How Everything Wrong Can Be Made Right* (New York: WaterBrook, 2016).

Jesus intercedes for the life of a woman who is about to be stoned to death, calling out the powerful oppressors in her life and their unjust religious interpretation of the law. He acts on justice and sets her free, extending shalom.

Jesus tells the Jewish leaders the story of a Samaritan man who he declares is a good neighbor because he shared shalom with someone he did not know.

We can extend shalom

Justice looks like extending shalom to my neighbor. Followers of Christ are called to the ministry of reconciliation, the ministry of shalom or justice. Each of us is called to seek the wholeness, safety, permanency, completeness, and restoration of our neighbors.

It's the body of Christ recognizing our Black neighbors' lives matter and calling on our communities and leaders to amend our laws and police practices that burden our neighbors.

Extending shalom is the church living by Mathew 25 and offering a place of safety and permanence to immigrants and refugees who seek a new home because we believe in the sanctity of life for people, whether they are born in our country or in other countries.

Justice will require us to listen, empathize, and sacrifice time, money, resources, and comfort so others who do not profit from the same privileges as we do also can have access to privileges like equitable education and health.

Justice begins by lending the microphone and giving voice to the marginalized, poor, and vulnerable to share their narratives and be empowered to lead in the restoration of justice in their communities.

Three years ago, justice was not served as I wanted it to be, but I saw a community—many of whom I had just met for the first time—advocating for the shalom of our immigrant community. It brought hope to my community that many who may not look like us or have similar stories are working to extend shalom actively to neighbors they do not know.

How are you extending shalom to your neighbors?

Anyra Cano was at the time this article originally appeared the coordinator for the Texas Baptist Women in Ministry, the academic coordinator of the Christian Latina Leadership Institute, and a youth minister at Iglesia Bautista Victoria en Cristo in Fort Worth. She is now the program and outreach director for Fellowship Southwest.

36

Justice looks and sounds like "just us"

Latisha Waters Hearne

The word and act of seeking justice are synonymous with issues surrounding racial inequity, police brutality, mass incarceration, and protests plaguing society.

As a Black woman working in a predominately white Christian space during an era of racial unrest, it is an exhausting effort to unpack the meaning of justice, what it is, and what it should look like for my community.

When Bryan Stevenson, the founder of the Equal Justice Initiative, attempted to answer a question about what justice is, he responded, "A constant struggle."[1] In that response alone, the word justice sounds weighty, heavy with angst about what to do and how to do it.

Moreover, the utterance of the word "justice" illustrates a personal battle about what is right and wrong. To ease the weight the term justice emits, I propose simplifying the concept and its meaning to two words: just us.

Sounding out the word

Before talking about where justice fits in the context of life, let us start by developing a basic understanding and familiarity with the word itself.

For a brief time as a child, I had a speech therapist assist me with learning to spell and read. I practiced pronouncing each

[1] https://www.al.com/spotnews/2012/11/an_interview_with_bryan _steven.html.

word, then visualizing its context, before adopting the full nature of its meaning.

My teacher repeatedly would say, "Just sound it out."

Initially, the thought of pronouncing a term I didn't fully comprehend frightened me. But after hearing the word spoken aloud, silently mumbling the word, then breaking it up into two or three parts, I could visualize it better, becoming comfortable and confident in my ability to say and understand the word.

Following that childhood practice, when I sound out the word "justice," then say it aloud a few times, I find myself morphing its syllables into a rhythmic chant, "Just us."

Most recently, I attended my first rally for justice, with a beautiful sea of people from all walks of life melodiously chanting, "No justice, no peace."

Again, at that moment, the words "just us" rang loud and clear. Justice is about us—"just us." Admittedly, while the outcry felt empowering and freeing in this solemn climate, I was struck by the overt connotation of the word "justice." The wordplay caught my attention.

Sounding out the heart

At the heart of justice is relationship—a mutual concern for others.

Justice is not just an act, an end, or a destination, but a deep feeling, a virtue, a visceral need to connect one to another in relationship, ensuring we all are safe and protected.

I grew up in a family of four siblings. We are so close in age that my mother and father did not permit us to attend events or frolic outside without being nearby each other. My parents continuously would say, "It's just us; you have to stick together." That sentiment signaled the pressing need for us to take care of one another.

Underpinning the duties of justice is the collective effort by the people to unite behind the elemental meaning of the word—a genuine concern for others.

In the Bible, it is no coincidence that the house of Justus was a place where both the Jews and Gentiles could meet to hear Paul preach the word of Jesus Christ (Acts 18:7).

Sounding out the personal

Fundamentally for me, justice begins with assessing personal feelings about righting wrongs for those within our immediate and extended communities.

In the wake of the murders of Breonna Taylor, Ahmaud Arbery, and George Floyd, there was an urgent call for justice during sixty days of protests. Simultaneously, there was a deafening silence on the part of justice,[2] particularly from Christian communities who admittedly struggle to find ways to engage in conversation around the topic.

I would attribute the conflicting behaviors to a lack of understanding about the essence of the word *justice*. Notwithstanding the complexities and nuances rooted in our quest for justice, consider my chant, "just us," as a way to see the humanity in the word.

Justice is purely about us—people standing in the gaps for one another. The late, great legal scholar and activist Derrick Bell reminded us that, as Christians, our call is to embrace, not exclude.

"We exist only in relation to our friends, family, life partners, co-workers, neighbors, strangers, even in relation to forces we cannot fully conceive of, let alone define. We are our relationships," Bell said.

Understanding the concept of justice through a much simpler lens of "just us" in relationships with one another is the first step to what the Lord requires of us in Micah 6:8, to act justly and to love mercy and walk humbly with God.

Sounding out the command

Justice is such a big word and is often overconceptualized by people who have benefited from imperfect systems struggling to uphold it. It is easier to enter into a dialogue about justice that results in action toward a more just community when we can simplify its meaning to the relational element of the word.

As we continue the conversation, let us start with a unified understanding that the meaning of justice lies within the word itself. It is just us working together on this arduous journey toward a fair and equitable society.

[2] https://abcnews.go.com/US/black-minneapolis-pastor-calls-white-evangelicals-speak-wake/story?id=71114467.

Be encouraged that justice is just about us here on earth fulfilling God's greatest commandments: "To love the Lord your God with all your heart and with all your soul and with all your mind. This is the first and greatest commandment. And the second is like it: love your neighbor as yourself" (Matthew 22:37–39).

Latisha Waters Hearne is a doctoral candidate at Dallas Baptist University and an advocate for racial justice. She serves on the board of Project Still I Rise Inc., a community-based, grassroots nonprofit organization focused on academic achievement, mentoring, and character development in underserved communities in Dallas.

37

For many, justice looks far away

Hon. Os Chrisman

When Barbara Jordan spoke to the US House of Representatives in regard to the selection of a Supreme Court justice, she said when she read those famous words from the Declaration of Independence—"We hold these truths to be self-evident, that all men are created equal, that they are endowed by their Creator with certain unalienable rights, that among them are life, liberty, and the pursuit of happiness"—she realized those words when written did not apply to her.

She did not qualify by sex, color, or background.

Today, we are reminded justice is not available to all based on their race, color, or origin.

All Christians should be asking why the Sermon on the Mount does not apply to all of our brothers and sisters.

What we profess vs. what we provide

Our society professes we believe in the rule of law. Due process is provided by law for all, yet we fail to deliver justice to the neediest in our communities. During summer 2020, we witnessed a young man murdered by vigilantes in the middle of the Bible belt and another choked to death by the knee of an officer, both without our beloved due process.

Justice looks far away for the families and loved ones of these victims.

Economic justice is very difficult for the homeless, the immigrant, the felon, and anyone different from the majority.

As a judge, I have tried to give justice with a good dose of mercy. I have that responsibility to everyone who comes into the courtroom.

The oath taken by every judge is to be impartial. In each case, I pray for wisdom, search the law and the lawyers' briefs, and try to do justice.

It is my hope we as a Christian community can have a view of what justice looks like in every phase of our lives.

Hon. Os Chrisman was a judge in family, probate, and district courts in Dallas County for thirteen years and a practicing attorney in Dallas for twenty-five years.

38

Justice looks like a widow not giving up

Myles Werntz

One of the most perplexing parables about the kingdom of God is found in Luke 18:1–8, where Jesus, teaching his disciples to pray, uses the example of a widow and a judge who can't be bothered to wake up.

The widow, Jesus tells us, is up against an arbiter of justice who loved neither God nor others, a man asleep to both the origins of justice in the world and to humanity. Jesus tells his disciples to pray like this widow—repetitively, persistently, openly.

Eventually, the widow gets the justice she seeks, the justice she is owed. There is no indication in the parable that her complaint is unwarranted, only that the judge is slow to answer her and, even then, does so out of exasperation. But what is so unsettling about the parable is the judge here is an analogy for *God*.

Wondering if the judge is asleep

You don't need to read very far into the Psalms to see this sentiment is close to Israel's heart. There, God is the one who has promised deliverance and justice, but the question always lingers. Maybe God has forgotten them, put them off, or, worst of all, remains asleep to our claims entirely.

Perhaps exile will be forever, our enemies will swallow us like the grave, and even our memories will be papered over. The gods of security, safety, and Mammon have set up shop all around us, and the powers of death and injustice win so frequently. The Psalms know this.

Our complaints for justice are very real complaints and deserve to be taken seriously, but the arc of justice moves so slowly. We live in a world where bread is needed daily; so, we pray for it daily, but the wheat will not be hurried.

Trusting the judge is awake

I do not think it is the case that God forgets us or loses track of us, but that the nights are very, very long. And in this parable, Jesus makes no move to defend the judge or to apologize for justice being slow in coming to the widow who deserves it.

What is shocking to us is Jesus encourages his disciples to keep asking and not to be silent. "And will not God bring about justice for his chosen ones, who cry out to him day and night? Will he keep putting them off? I tell you, he will see that they get justice, and quickly. However, when the Son of Man comes, will he find faith on the earth?" (Luke 18:7–8).

The disciples are to be those who, in faith, continue to ask for God to be true to the promises of God even when it seems as if the judge is asleep. The Psalms know this well. The people of God keep asking, keep pushing, keep speaking the promises of God back to God.

For God is the only one who can give justice, and God is the one who Scripture tells us will continue to give justice, even when it seems all is lost. Being God's people means we are the people encouraged to keep asking for it long after the night has come and those around us would rather we be quiet and go to sleep as well.

Myles Werntz is director of Baptist studies and associate professor of theology at Abilene Christian University, where he leads the Baptist Studies Center in the Graduate School of Theology. He is the author and editor of seven books in theology and ethics, including From Isolation to Community: A Renewed Vision for Christian Life Together *(2022).*

39

Justice looks like putting out the fire

Roy J. Cotton

What if your neighbor's house was on fire? After calling 911, hearing the sirens blaring louder, coming closer, suddenly, to your horror, you see them stop at the beginning of your block and commence spraying every house instead of the house on fire.

How would you feel regarding such disregard? Disappointed? Marginalized? Horrified? These are putting it mildly. What if the fire department answered your urgent concern with the tepid response that they wanted to equalize resources with other houses?

This scenario is being played out across the country. Peaceful protesters are voicing deep frustration with the high number of Black lives that have been lost due to injustice. There have been too many indications of a system that has gone badly wrong.

A plethora of injustices against people of color dominate the news weekly. What will it take to awaken a sense of urgency to the evils of systemic racism?

"Black Lives Matter" reached accelerated crescendos of *fortissimo* decibels last summer. People are urgently crying out for social justice now. They are marching with megaphones while speaking truth to power, "Enough is enough!" "We're sick and tired of being sick and tired!"

The situation is desperate. It is an emergency. The house is on fire!

The Bible's view of justice

What does justice look like? It looks like *imago Dei*—all people created in the image of God (Genesis 1:27).

Justice is an attribute of God. God is a God of justice. "Righteousness and justice are the foundation of his throne" (Psalm 97:2).

The Bible is replete with references to how people of God must be just and fair in all our dealings with other people made in God's image.

Notice: Justice calls for action according to a psalm of Asaph: "Provide justice for the needy and the fatherless; uphold the rights of the oppressed and the destitute. Rescue the poor and needy; save them from the power of the wicked" (Psalm 82:3–4).

Where is the church?

So, where is the church? The church cannot be silent while African Americans and other people of color are demanding justice in the face of systemic racism.

The church represents Jesus Christ in the world. Our mission is that of reconciling the world to Christ. We are Christ's ambassadors (2 Corinthians 5:20).

It is very dismissive of the church to see injustices and respond with callous complacency that "all lives matter." Yes, they do, but *our* house is on fire.

We are compassionate Christ followers. The world is watching our reaction. Action is needed individually and collectively. "Who knows? Perhaps, you have come to your royal position for such a time as this" (Esther 4:14b).

The late twentieth-century theologian and martyr Dietrich Bonhoeffer stated, "Silence in the face of evil is itself evil. God will not hold us guiltless. Not to speak is to speak. Not to act is to act."

The prolific twentieth-century theologian C. S. Lewis stated, "One of the most cowardly things ordinary people do is to shut their eyes to the facts."

Seeing value and worth in all people

Justice looks like people who see value and worth in all people. Justice does something about a system that victimizes innocents.

Social justice takes Christ's words seriously in relieving the atrocities hurting "the least of these" (Matthew 25:40).

Mother Teresa was asked once how she served in such desperate conditions in Calcutta. Her answer: "I see the face of Jesus in every child."

Friends, that is what justice looks like. We must see Jesus in every face. Eric Garner, Breonna Taylor, Ahmaud Arbery, George Floyd, and too many others have been silenced unjustly. Their lives mattered.

Reform is demanded to fix a broken system. What about the sanctity of life?

Remember the late US Rep. John Robert Lewis' impassioned query that awakens our immediate action, "If not us, then who? If not now, then when?"

The Declaration of Independence proclaims, "We hold these truths to be self-evident, that *all men are created equal*." The fact is Black Lives Matter is not about special treatment, but equal justice.

Realize your potential in this urgent matter. The next house that's on fire could be yours. What would you want others to do?

Jesus' command, what we call the Golden Rule, is this: "Therefore, whatever you want others to do for you, do also the same for them" (Matthew 7:12).

What does justice look like to you?

Dr. Roy J. Cotton retired after serving Texas Baptists for twenty-one years, first as a church starting consultant and then as director of African American Ministries. Roy is serving as an independent contractor coordinating the Ambassador Program. He and his wife Inez are parents of two talented sons and proud grandparents of four.

40

Justice looks like my bookshelves

Jean Surratt Humphreys

Justice looks like my bookshelves. My bookshelves at home are full of my favorite books, the ones you grab when you're trying to remember something or the ones you grab just for comfort.

My bookshelves also contain photographs of the women in my family who have taught me what justice looks like.

Justice in women's lives

My mother appears in her wedding dress, looking forward to starting a family. She grew up the daughter of a single mother in Odessa and saw the New Deal bring her family out of poverty. Her mother worked for the Works Progress Administration as a seamstress. One brother worked for the Civilian Conservation Corps, and after World War II, the other went to Southern Methodist University on the GI bill.

She went to the College of Marshall and graduated from East Texas Baptist College on academic scholarships. As she grew up, the public schools gave her an incredible education, and she was part of their annual honor tour for seniors visiting Montreal. She saw the strength of both a government and a church that cared for her family.

My aunt appears in one of the photographs with her Cessna Piper Cub, which she flew with girlfriends beginning in the 1950s, scouring the Southwest in "Powder Puff Derbies." She traveled and worked and helped to raise her nieces and nephew, marrying when she was forty-nine. Her marriage modeled a partnership, as my Uncle George joined Auntie Laurie and her girlfriends on their trips.

During her time as the head statistician at Blue Cross Blue Shield, my aunt's sense of justice and fairness tolerated no slothfulness but had much grace.

My daughter is in two photographs on my bookshelves, one in her wedding dress and the other in a blue jean jacket from high school. She's now a public-school teacher, wife, and mother of two amazing children.

Her generation has a different sense of justice. Her justice is not just for her children, but for all children. Her justice recognizes the privileges we've had as white women.

We all have stories of being hushed in church, of being told leadership is male and God is a man. But my daughter sees even more clearly, past the "benevolent patriarchy" of our church culture into what life is like for others.

"Weathering" of racial discrimination

She has two brothers, and when those brothers were teenagers, I did not have to worry about them being shot by the police if they got in trouble. I may have worried a few times about a call from the school or a police station, but I was not fearing for their lives.

What would it be like to have to worry about them constantly, that they might be pulled over for nothing or for a minor infraction and pay with their lives?

During this pandemic, we are worried and stressed, having to make constant decisions about what to do and what is safe. I've asked myself, "Is this some of what life may be like as a Black woman, who experiences years of stress?"

This cumulative stress is the "weathering" of racial discrimination throughout life, having to think, "Is this safe, and is my son safe?"

"Weathering"—a term coined by Arline Geronimus in 1992—explains why infants born to late-adolescent Black women were healthier than those of Black women in their 20s, while the opposite was and still is true in white women.

These disparities are not explained by income or education, yet they still exist. Indeed, "a middle-class, college-educated Black woman is more likely than a non-Hispanic white woman with a high school diploma to give birth prematurely."[1]

As Baptists, we often focus on individual sin and salvation, but we also are part of the larger world. Our actions reinforce the social policies that perpetuate the injustice of weathering.

We reinforce it when we want the best schools for our children and merely adequate schools for others. We reinforce it when our children have good health care, but others wait for days. We reinforce it when we ask friends to help our children find jobs, but others go without this social capital.

Galatians 3:28 calls for a more just world, where "there is neither Jew nor Greek, there is neither slave nor free, there is no male and female, for you are all one in Christ Jesus."

My prayer is, as my mother taught me, that we do justice, love kindness, and walk humbly with our God.

Jean Surratt Humphreys' first experience in the Baptist world was going to Camp Paisano as a toddler. Since then she obtained a BA from East Texas Baptist College, an MA from Baylor, and a PhD from UTA. She has taught sociology at Dallas Baptist University for thirty years. She resides in Arlington, Texas, and tries to keep up with her husband, children, and grandchildren.

[1] https://digitalscholarship.unlv.edu/cgi/viewcontent.cgi?article=1796&context=jhdrp.

41

I never knew I was Black

Levi Bedilu

I never knew I was Black until I came to America. Growing up in the streets of Addis Ababa, Ethiopia, "Black" was how my grandfather liked his coffee. In a country where everyone looks like me, my skin tone never mattered.

My culture did not prepare me for what to expect once we touched down at DFW Airport.

I always will remember my confusion on that first day of school, watching my dad fill in the section marked "race." Why was the color of my skin important? Why didn't it ask where I was from?

My parents tried to warn me, "We are new here. Don't be talkative. Listen, and don't ask questions."

So, I never asked; I never spoke. Instead, when asked every year at enrollment what my race was, I checked "other" as a form of silent protest.

Regardless of what I checked, America had no interest in my identity. I was Black.

Black in America is not a color

Black in America is not a color. It is a brand that defines where you fit in American culture. It defines what type of music you supposedly listen to or what kind of lifestyle you're assumed to live.

Black is the neighborhood you didn't want to live in because it was deemed "unsafe."

Black is not a color. Black is an expectation of mediocrity.

That lesson was taught in schools with more regularity than my math courses. Report card day always came with a bit of shock from administrators who began to see me as an exception to being Black.

To be Black implied aggression in everyday situations. I remember staring into the eyes of my principal after trying to convince her I wasn't fighting with another student. She responded by saying she couldn't contradict what a veteran teacher told her. She already had reached her decision.

Church history in America

If you study American history, slavery and racism didn't just influence American culture, economics, or politics. It defined this nation for generations.

History tells us the American church often found itself as a silent bystander or, worse, an active participant in the atrocities.

The first slaves were beaten six days a week and told to worship the God of their masters on the seventh. Forced into Christianity and on the receiving end of an evil racial divide, the Black church came into existence. Not by choice, but out of survival and faith in Christ.

The white American church was unable to recognize the *imago Dei*—the image of God in every living human, including in Black bodies—and therefore persecuted generations of Black Christians.

The political and racial segregation mirrored the spiritual segregation of America. Over hundreds of years, white and Black churches evolved to become completely separate bodies of believers.

Now, here I am, an Ethiopian American living in the twenty-first century expected to attend a Black church. This is what it means to be a Black believer in America.

Sadly, I don't believe the American church looks any different today than it did in 1850. Every Sunday morning, you can expect Black to mean a multitude of things, but it is especially a description of where someone should gather with other Christians.

Hope for unity in the church

How can a country be won for Christ by a church that looks as divided as the society it lives in?

The biblical path to justice I see and pray for begins within the church. My hope is every pastor and elder of a predominately white church will look across their city and reconcile with the Black churches around them—gathering and praising Christ together, uplifting one another in perfect love.

My hope and prayer are they will recognize the *imago Dei* of every Black body and resist the negative adjectives and prejudicial definitions of Black ascribed by the history of America.

There is nothing under heaven that can't be changed by a unified and transformed church.

Would you begin praying for that today? Would you ask the Lord to make a way for us to unite?

Then, if you are a member of a local church, may I ask you for one more thing? Ask your pastors, elders, or other leaders to do the same.

Levi Bedilu is an experienced finance analyst who has worked with multiple Fortune 100 companies. Outside of working in corporate finance, he is driven to proclaim Christ with his wife wherever Christ takes them. They love to serve and speak in multiethnic churches and spaces. He is the son of Pastor Bedilu Yirga, senior pastor of Ethiopian Evangelical Baptist Church in Garland.

42

Justice looks like a Toni Morrison plot

Michelle L. Henry

Justice looks like the masterfully constructed, wonderfully fulfilling, yet strangely elusive plot of any novel from Toni Morrison's rich and complex canon, which so deftly explores the depth and breadth of the African American experience.

During my junior year in high school, I was introduced to the riotous, revolutionary, and redeeming literary imagination of one of our nation's most gifted writers.

After thirty years of peering into the lives of her characters, traversing the grounds they walked, haunting the places they inhabited, and interpreting the meaning of their experiences—often fraught with tension caused by their individual and collective attempts to make a life in a violent, unfair, and inhospitable society—I have found that a profoundly nuanced definition of justice has emerged.

Painting justice in words

In the "quiet as it's kept" world Morrison envisions in *The Bluest Eye*, justice sounds like the whispered intercessory prayer of one Black girl countering the silent but destructive wish of another, who believes possessing the bluest eye might garner her the love and affection she craves.

Justice reverberates through Baby Suggs' sermon in *Beloved*, preached at the clearing to the recently freed—by virtue of legal writ or personal declaration—as she admonishes them to love, honor, and value themselves, for to do so is the "prize." In so doing, she empowers them to reclaim the lives stolen from them and to see themselves as beloved.

Justice dismantles the "house that race built," the one constructed on the idea that our nation's strength, power, and longevity are contingent on its ability and willingness to either "wrest dominion" from those it deems unworthy of its promise, as Morrison writes in *A Mercy*, or to deny entry to those who seek refuge and the shelter of its bountiful dream.

In the America Morrison imagines—in novels such as *Paradise* and *Home*—justice bends the arc of our moral imagination toward paradise, where home is defined as a place in which all its inhabitants feel both "free and situated."

As she is now a member of that great ancestral throng, justice looks like the legacy of my literary mother.

Seeing justice as faith in action

Justice looks like the most personal commitment one can make to the public good, righteously defending the vulnerable and rightfully pursuing the fulfillment of our highest moral and ethical principles.

As a person of faith, I always have been drawn, like a moth to a flame, to those great men and women who have committed themselves not only to being honest, fair, and just but to *doing* justice.

When we seek to do good, to be good, and to make good, even if and especially when it requires great personal sacrifice, we create the change we desire to see.

In this instance, justice looks like the liberating gospel of Christ in motion. It is what we witness when we turn our revolutionary faith—our inward belief in that most sacred and salvific gospel—outward toward those who need it and speak truth to the powers that threaten human life and dignity.

In the plaintive cries and early quests for freedom so painstakingly captured in the narratives of Frederick Douglass, Harriet Jacobs, and Solomon Northrup, I discovered what it means to have hope in the midst of despair.

From the historical and sociological perspectives of W. E. B. Du Bois and Alain Locke, I learned of the spiritual "strivings," intellectual aims, and artistic aspirations of a people not only wed to the idea of equality but also dedicated to its manifestation in every sphere of endeavor.

Through the essays and records of Ida B. Wells Barnett, I am reminded of some of the earliest protests against the extralegal, state-ignored, and sometimes sanctioned lynchings of Black bodies that lend context and credibility to our current, righteous indignation concerning the police brutality so often visited upon African Americans.

Though Dr. Martin Luther King Jr. may be known most widely for his beautiful "dream," for those of us who have not forgotten the totality of his message, he always will be remembered for the way he awakened us to the evils of racism, poverty, and war.

In the wake of the passing of two heroes of the civil rights era—the Honorable Congressman John Robert Lewis and Rev. C. T. Vivian, an activist, organizer, and author—who both carried the baton unwaveringly for human rights well into the twenty-first century, justice demands we vote, protest, and march on as they did until all that remains imbalanced is made equitable.

Be firm in this resolve until justice looks like a new day dawning.

For further reading:

By Toni Morrison: *The Bluest Eye*; *Beloved*; *A Mercy*; "Home," in *The House That Race Built*.
By W. E. B. DuBois: *The Souls of Black Folk*.
By Dr. Martin Luther King Jr.: "I Have a Dream," "America's Chief Moral Dilemma."

Dr. Michelle L. Henry is a professor of English who loves reading, paper crafting, and sharing life with her family and close friends.

43

Justice is something we learn and practice

Wes Keyes

The first time I truly began to understand what the word *justice* meant to me and my faith in Christ was under a pecan tree during my seminary days in Waco.

John Perkins, the civil rights activist, Christian leader, and founder of the Christian Community Development Association, sat me down under that tree, and over a meal of cracked pecans, he told me what it was like to grow up as a Black man in our shared home state of Mississippi.

John was in Waco after the annual CCDA convention. He was coming to preach at Mission Waco's Church Under the Bridge, and I was tasked with hosting him. This led to the opportunity to dialogue about the truth of justice that would change my life.

When I learned about justice

I am embarrassed to say this was the first time I made the effort to listen to a story like this. For me, growing up in the church in the Deep South did not offer me the opportunity to hear the heroic stories of men like John Perkins and the justice they sought. I never was taught that my faith should move me toward fighting for the rights of others and for justice-centered initiatives.

During my time in seminary, I started exploring Scripture passages and theology about race, justice, equality, and mercy. I was astonished to see the Bible come alive as a repository of justice-centered stories and commandments.

Passages like the following convicted me and caused me to repent:

> Learn to do right; seek justice.
> Defend the oppressed.
> Take up the cause of the fatherless;
> plead the case of the widow. (Isaiah 1:17)

> "The Spirit of the Lord is on me,
> because he has anointed me
> to proclaim good news to the poor.
> He has sent me to proclaim freedom for the prisoners
> and recovery of sight for the blind,
> to set the oppressed free,
> to proclaim the year of the Lord's favor." (Luke 4:18–19)

> There is neither Jew nor Gentile, neither slave nor free, nor
> is there male and female, for you are all one in Christ Jesus.
> (Galatians 3:28)

It was because of these encounters that I set out on a career of seeking, teaching, and doing justice in the church and now do so as a leader of a historic Dallas nonprofit.

Where I practice justice

At Brother Bill's Helping Hand, we serve the men, women, and children who are represented in these passages. Many are oppressed, fatherless, widowed, poor, formerly incarcerated, or in poor health.

Because we believe all are created in God's image, we are compelled to provide our neighbors with the essentials of life: food for the hungry; care for their mental and physical health; and job training, education, and Christian discipleship.

We do this not out of a secular humanism compulsion, but rather from a place of deep devotion to the God who has taught us that the *imago Dei* exists in all humans, regardless of skin color, social status, wealth, health, or past.

As believers, if we ignore this conviction, the Spirit of Christ is not in us.

The lingering effect of our words

As I prepared this article, I reread several past articles and sermons from white pastors here in Dallas during the era of desegregation. It was an important but difficult exercise. To hear these men of God say hurtful and untrue words about their understanding of God and people of different races was excruciatingly painful.

Even today, it brings me great pain to read and hear articles, sermons, and social media posts from Christians—more specifically, white Christians—who simply do not see these themes in the Bible or see these problems in our current climate.

Christians, and unfortunately many of my Baptist brothers and sisters, have been on the wrong side of God's plan for humanity for many years.

This was not 150 or 200 years ago; this was 50 to 60 years ago. While some of these pastors repented, others let that legacy of bigotry live on within their churches and congregations. They let it fester and be fueled by new narratives of fear and hate, narratives I still hear echoes of today.

Embrace a redeemed narrative

We as Christians must embrace a redeemed narrative, one not sullied by secular thought but rather supported by Scripture, influenced by the Holy Spirit, and modeled by Jesus.

The neighbors, staff members, and community we know and love are disproportionately vulnerable to current injustice. This is an unavoidable truth. We have witnessed stories of hardship, abuse, and suffering at the hands of those in power for far too long.

But we are not dismayed or deterred. At Brother Bill's Helping Hand, we intend to continue to unify the body of Christ by loving our neighbors as ourselves.

Wes Keyes is Chief Executive Officer of Brother Bill's Helping Hand. He has worked in impoverished communities in Waco, Dallas, rural Mississippi, Haiti, Turkey, Guatemala, and elsewhere.

44

What justice looks like depends on where you're standing

Scott Collins

Robben Island is located in Table Bay, about four miles north of Cape Town, South Africa. Nestled between the Atlantic Ocean and Table Mountain, Cape Town is one of the most picturesque cities in the world.

If you take Highway 27 around to the north and look back toward Cape Town, the view is breathtaking except for Robben Island, which stands between you and the city.

That is the view I took in more than thirty-five years ago as a young man. It is a vision etched in my memory because of the beauty of the setting. But also because as I stood on the shore of the ocean and looked back at Cape Town, I was keenly aware I was looking at Nelson Mandela's prison.

Imprisoned for twenty-seven years—eighteen of them on Robben Island—because of his opposition to white-ruled South Africa's legal system of apartheid, I'm sure Nelson Mandela's view was starkly different from mine.

For two years, as a Southern Baptist missionary journeyman, I lived in South Africa's neighbor to the north, Botswana. During that time, I traveled throughout South Africa. Now, years later, I struggle with the privilege I enjoyed as a white person.

Seeing justice through another's eyes

Most white people in America and around the world have no idea what justice looks like through the eyes of people of color.

What does justice look like? It depends on your perspective. It's like two people who witness a car accident and give different accounts because of where they were standing.

In *White Fragility*, Robin DiAngelo writes, "For most whites, racism is like murder: the concept exists, but someone has to commit it in order for it to happen."[1]

In other words, if you're white, you have no clue racism is happening right now. But for Black people, it's always there. It's all a matter of perspective and how you see the world—and how the world sees you.

One of the greatest sources of tension between Jesus and the religious leaders of his day grew out of their different perspectives. They didn't understand Jesus and had no idea what to do with him because their perspectives were so different.

Why would Jesus heal a woman on the Sabbath? they asked indignantly. From Jesus' perspective, why wouldn't you? He scolded them for treating their oxen and donkeys better than they treated the poor (Luke 13:10–17).

Jesus' constant pattern was to affirm the value of the people he ministered to rather than the human laws he may have been violating.

Stand where another stands

We white people look indignantly at peaceful protests happening around the world and scold the protesters. It's a convenient way to ignore the issue.

But look at it from the perspective of a Black person. Walk in the shoes of a Black man who drives his car in fear of being stopped for DWB—driving while Black.

A Black friend I work with at Buckner International opened my eyes recently to his view. Referring to Black Lives Matter, he said, "Of course all lives matter, just like all houses matter. But if it's your house on fire, then only your house matters."

---

[1]   Robin DiAngelo, *White Fragility: Why It's So Hard for White People to Talk about Racism* (Boston: Beacon, 2018), 72.

From his perspective as a Black man, all lives matter, but because of racial injustice, we need to focus on Black lives until we put out the fire.

Years after being released from Robben Island and serving as president of South Africa, Mandela wrote in his autobiography, *Long Walk to Freedom*, about the time a white Methodist minister held Sunday services for prisoners on the island. The minister implied it was the Black Africans who needed to reconcile themselves with the whites who put them in prison for their dissent.

"I noticed that Eddie Daniels (another prisoner) could take it no longer," Mandela wrote. "'You're preaching reconciliation to the wrong people,' Daniels said. 'We've been seeking reconciliation for the last 75 years.'"

What does justice look like? It depends on your perspective. Maybe it's time we all saw it from Jesus' perspective.

Scott Collins is senior vice president of communications for Buckner International.

45

Justice looks like stepping in and seeking solutions for others

Gus Reyes

Micah 6:8 challenges us to do justice. What does that look like?

Justice looks like my dad explaining how I will have to endure the consequences of my actions. He spent several years in law enforcement and had a real knack for catching me at misbehavior. He worked hard to make my consequences "memorable."

He also wanted me to know there would be different consequences when I broke different house rules. Not all rules were the same. He wanted me to know he would be fair with me and that I someday would have to help my own children understand there were consequences and/or rewards for actions and decisions made. This was my introduction to justice.

Rules for the household

Justice was a set of rules that applied to all in the household. Following the rules resulted in all kinds of fun and joyful experiences. Breaking the rules was entirely different and "memorable."

After a short while, a little brother joined the family. The day came when I learned another facet of justice. I forgot to take care of my brother in the manner I was taught. I did not look after his safety needs or his welfare. He could not look after himself. He could not even feed himself. I got in trouble for not looking after him.

Through this experience with my brother, my parents taught me the importance of looking after those who literally were not able to look after themselves. In his case, he was just too young, but the point remains the same. There would be situations in life when it would be important for me to look after the needs and rights of others for the sake of justice and fairness.

Justice looks like caring for others. Justice involves me being aware when the needs of others are not being met and that I should do good by working to help others.

A lesson in fairness

One day, I was told how my dad would not get a promotion at work because of his ethnicity. This was the day I learned about fairness and just opportunities for all. He did not have fair opportunity to earn an income. He would train his future supervisor and was passed over for a promotion. The lack of justice and a fair opportunity impacted our entire family.

Dad received a call from California. Mr. Rocky Fuertez said his employer was interested in results and not the complexion of someone's skin. So, off to California we went. We left all family, friends, and church ties behind for dad's opportunity to provide for his family.

I recognized this was not fair; it was not just. However, we learned to appreciate employers who would give all persons an opportunity for success dependent only upon results.

The family table talk included the importance of respecting people who looked different than us and the importance of working to give everyone an opportunity to succeed.

Justice looks like Jesus

When I attended an English-speaking Baptist church in Rialto, California, Pastor Leonard Roten taught us about a biblical perspective on justice and how God did not give us what we deserve for our sins.

Pastor Roten, along with church leaders like Sam Edwards, Doug Mitchell, and my parents, introduced me to God's grace and mercy. They helped me understand Jesus paid the ultimate price for my sins, helping me when I could not help myself. I was moved by these biblical ideas and dedicated myself to learn more about God's justice and salvation by faith in Jesus.

How thankful I am justice looks like Jesus paying for my sins and giving me salvation.

God's justice looks like the Scripture stating, "All have sinned and fall short of the glory of God" and that he reconciled me to himself through his Son Jesus. I am so thankful God stepped in and provided a solution for my sin.

This picture of justice calls me to step in and seek solutions for those experiencing injustice so no one has to move across the country to find equal opportunity. It calls me to be on the lookout for gaps in fairness for those who need help and aren't able to help themselves. It calls on me to act for the benefit of others. This is what justice looks like to me.

Dr. Gus Reyes was the director of Texas Baptists' Christian Life Commission and serves as the director of Hispanic Partnerships at Dallas Baptist University. He continues to look for opportunities to help those in need with appropriate solutions. He has been married to Leticia Lozano Reyes for more than forty-four years, and they are blessed with grandchildren.

46

Justice looks like all our responsibility
Rev. Debra F. Bell

> Righteousness and justice are the foundation of your throne; love and
> faithfulness go before you. (Psalms 89:14)

The word *justice* carries with it the concepts of fairness, respect,
equity, peace, impartiality, and decency.[1]

These concepts are implicit in the US Constitution. All citizens
have the right to life, liberty, and the pursuit of happiness based on
the US Declaration of Independence.

These implicit concepts of freedom have been denied to Black
Americans. Consider that the slave trade began in America in
1619. The end of slavery was mandated in 1865 by the Thirteenth
Amendment to the Constitution. From 1877 to 1964, Black Americans were subject to the segregationist rules of Jim Crow laws
that denied justice[2]—fairness, respect, equity, peace, impartiality,
and decency—thus treating these citizens differently than other
Americans.

I do believe, however, there are places to begin the process.

Where to start

There must be a restructuring of how laws are applied disproportionately to Black Americans and other people of color. The
church universal must speak out on issues of injustice, not only
Black and brown church leaders. Finally, individuals who profess

[1] https://www.dictionary.com/browse/justice.
[2] https://www.history.com/topics/black-history/slavery.

faith in Christ must hold one another accountable for justice and righteousness.

There must be a restructuring of how laws disproportionately disadvantage Black Americans and other people of color. Over three thousand lynchings of Black Americans occurred from 1882 to 1968. Within this era, there were homes and churches burned and Blacks murdered without any judicial or legal remedy.[3]

The Civil Rights Act of 1964 ended the segregationist Jim Crow laws and, in essence, gave civil liberties to Americans who had been denied those liberties. Even so, beginning with the murder of Trayvon Martin on February 26, 2012, through to May 25, 2020, the eyes of the world have been focused on modern-day lynching, as seen in the televised murder of George Floyd at the knee of a public servant, a police officer.[4]

Politicians use redlining disproportionately to leave Black Americans and other people of color without funding from banks to purchase new homes in different areas of a city or to get approval for loans to repair their homes.[5] The vestiges of this practice remain in effect across the United States.

I suggest justice must look like something we have never seen or experienced before as a country and people.

Task forces could be established to monitor how civil liberties are being upheld in industries and penalties applied when infractions occur.

Speaking out

The church universal must join Black and brown church leaders in speaking out on issues of injustice.

In an interview on Trinity Broadcasting Network, Tony Evans spoke out on the silence of white church leaders on the plight of Black Americans being killed in the streets over the last five years. Evans suggested the absence of equity among God's rule has been

[3]   http://archive.tuskegee.edu/archive/handle/123456789/511.

[4]   https://www.usnews.com/news/top-news/articles/2020-06-10/protests-to-change-the-whole-wide-world-following-floyds-funeral.

[5]   https://www.marketplace.org/2020/04/16/inequality-by-design-how-redlining-continues-to-shape-our-economy/.

absent and silent. He further stated, "People will affirm things they believe in morally but not speak on things that involve the dignity of other people."[6]

Evans urged the church and her leaders to adopt not just a "nine-month life agenda, but a whole-life agenda" that agrees Black lives matter. Only then do we represent God's agenda as the church, he said.

The responsibility of speaking out, educating, and teaching is not only on those being wronged; all those who believe in justice must speak out. All our leaders are needed to advocate for fairness, respect, equity, peace, impartiality, and decency.

Justice involves all of us

Martin Luther King Jr. said, "Injustice anywhere is a threat to justice everywhere. We are caught in an inescapable network of mutuality, tied in a single garment of destiny. Whatever affects one directly, affects all indirectly."[7] This speaks to my final suggested action.

We the people must take responsibility if there is to be change. I can—you can—no longer afford to sit by idly as injustice continues.

It will require us to hold each other accountable to speak up and speak out when we witness or experience injustice.

God requires not only righteousness from us but justice also. It is our responsibility as we enact the Scripture that says, "By this all people will know that you are my disciples, if you have love for one another" (John 13:35).

Rev. Debra F. Bell is owner of and senior consultant for P3Coaching and Consulting. Debra is a certified coach, trainer, and speaker with John Maxwell Team. She currently serves at The Church Without Walls and as the assistant director of career services at Houston Christian University.

---

[6]   https://watch.tbn.org/videos/hd-p031220.
[7]   https://www.biography.com/news/martin-luther-king-famous-quotes.

47

Justice looks like awakening

Nataly Mora Sorenson

I have witnessed injustices in my life.

During my time in college, I comforted a young lady who had mustered the courage to press charges against the young men who sexually assaulted her only to find a system that did not defend her or find her case important.

I witnessed children being taken away from their mother because the mother did not have the money, citizenship status, or resources to defend herself.

When I think of justice, I often think of the justice system, and the times it has failed those it should have protected.

But what about me? When have I failed to protect the vulnerable in my community?

What about you? When have you failed to protect your neighbor?

Awareness of others and oneself

I am a social work student, and I am a pastor. As social workers in training, we are taught to develop the skills of tuning in to our clients and of self-awareness. Tuning in develops empathy. You put yourself in your client's shoes. Self-awareness is the ability to recognize your beliefs, attitudes, biases, emotions, values, strengths, weaknesses, and what motivates your behavior.

As a pastor, I encourage my congregation to love their neighbor as themselves. I encourage reflection, confession, and repentance.

Tuning in to the other and self-awareness pair well with the Christian teaching of loving our neighbor. Liberation theology calls this conscientization—the dynamic of awakening, of helping people become aware that they have the power to bring about change.

Justice looks like awakening—awakening ourselves to the plea of others, tuning in to the pain of others, developing empathy, and doing something about it.

Justice is an action

In Spanish, to do righteous acts is to do *justicia*—justice. Miguel A. De La Torre, in his article "Breaking Barriers: Reading the Bible in Spanish," writes, "For English speakers, righteous means morally right or justifiable, acting in an upright, moral way. The definition implies an action that can be performed privately."[1]

But *righteous* in Spanish is *justice*. And justice "only occurs in community . . . [and] cannot be reduced to a private expression of faith; it is a public action," he continues.

Good Samaritan displays justice

The parable of the good Samaritan tells the story of a man robbed, beaten, and left "half dead" beside the road. A Jewish priest and then a Levite stumble upon the man, but each continues on his way.

A Samaritan also stumbles upon the man, stops, and helps the injured Jewish man. One should note: Samaritans and Jews were enemies. However, the Samaritan interrupted his journey and went out of his way to help the injured Jew. He took him to an inn, stayed with him, and when he left the inn, gave the innkeeper enough money to provide for the care of the injured man.

Jesus then asked an expert of the law, "Which of these three do you think was a neighbor to the man who fell into the hands of robbers?"

"The expert in the law replied, 'The one who had mercy on him.'"

"Jesus told him, 'Go and do likewise'" (Luke 10:36–37).

This parable expresses justice. It shows us justice is a public action. It shows justice in awakening oneself to the plea of another, self-awareness, and action.

---

[1] https://goodfaithmedia.org/breaking-barriers-reading-the-bible-in -spanish-cms-15706/.

The Samaritan man tuned in by empathizing with the injured Jew left on the side of the road. He must have become self-aware by recognizing his own beliefs, biases, emotions, values, strengths, and weaknesses. He was a Samaritan, and we can assume the injured man was a Jew.

The Samaritan must have recognized the racial tension and the power of resources he had—a donkey to carry the man to an inn, bandages, oil, wine, and just enough money to take care of the man—and that he may have to reimburse the innkeeper for any additional expenses.

In the story, we see the Samaritan man put justice into practice by doing something about the man left on the side of the road.

Practicing justice

In life, we will stumble upon injustices like the injured man left beside the road. The question is, Will we fail to protect our neighbor? Will we allow ourselves to awaken to the plea of another?

Despite the differences we may have with the other—like the Samaritan and the Jew in the parable—will we use our power and our resources to do *justicia*?

Nataly Mora Sorenson earned a master of divinity and master of social work at Baylor University and Truett Theological Seminary in 2021. She is currently the executive director of Gaston Christian Center in Dallas, an ordained minister, and a licensed social worker for the state of Texas.

48

Justice looks like other Mexicans

Jesse Rincones

"You're not like other Mexicans."

This was how the assistant to the director of missions greeted me after speaking at a youth camp service. Did he intend this to be a compliment? Did those words sound as weird as I felt hearing them?

He mentioned something about the way I communicated, but the rest of the conversation is hazy. The only other thing I remember was a tangential recommendation that I read Dallas Willard.

That phrase has periodically boomeranged back into my mind. Sometimes, it led me to moments of exploration. Sometimes, it caused self-analysis. Sometimes, it caused anger or frustration. Other times, I struggled to understand the perspective of how people see "Mexicans" and "other Mexicans."

One of the ricochets of that phrase led me to a confession.

Any other Mexican

Years after that post-sermon conversation, I recalled that phrase while in my first full-time pastorate.

As I was sitting with several pastors from the small town of Hereford, Texas, our conversation turned to the growing trend of dressing casually in church. I mentioned that, except for funerals and weddings, I rarely wore a suit and tie to church and definitely did not do so during the week.

A first-generation immigrant pastor, dark-skinned and short in stature, who appeared to be in his 60s, said in Spanish, "I have to wear a suit and tie every day and wherever I go. Otherwise, I get treated just like 'any other Mexican.'"

My heart broke. I wondered how many times he suffered humiliation or abuse based solely on his appearance—how the Father had knit him in his mother's womb. How many times was he laughed at because of how he pronounced words? Or presumed ignorant just because of his accent? Had he automatically come under heightened suspicion in stores or by authorities due to the color of his skin? Was he ever subjected to physical violence?

It was abundantly clear his first-generation, Spanish-dominant Mexican-immigrant experience was not my third-generation, English-dominant Texan experience.

Kat-Kits and privilege

Serving as a Baptist Student Ministry summer missionary at a migrant center in Hermitage, Arkansas, I was given the responsibility of taking five or six boys to kids' camp. We were the only Hispanics in the entire camp for the week.

I joined two other volunteers overseeing the snack cabin, and kids from the migrant center came to the window and ordered. The last one asked for a chocolate bar—a "Kat-Kit." After the kids left, the teens busted out laughing, "Did you hear him? He called it a 'Kat-Kit' instead of a Kit-Kat!"

I didn't know how to engage them; so, I started with a grammar lesson. I explained to the teens that in Spanish, adjectives usually come after the noun, which is the opposite of the general practice in English.

A native Spanish speaker is thinking, "Día caliente," and if not privy to the rule, literally will translate it to "day hot." I told them this probably didn't play a role in the "Kat-Kit" flub, but they should be aware of it for future reference.

Their response was, "You're Mexican?" I explained that my grandparents were from Mexico.

They saw me differently. And, because of it, they treated me differently.

My confession? I have experienced this privilege regularly in my life.

Is it the lighter skin? Or the fact I'm six feet, two inches tall? Was it my lack of an accent? Or, maybe it was that I conveniently dropped in conversation the fact that I went to law school.

Whatever it was, I know I was asked to sit at tables where less-acculturated Hispanic leaders were not invited. I did not suffer the same frustration and humiliation at border crossings as my darker-skinned pastor friend, who has more degrees than I do.

Whether sincerely or not, I was treated with the kind of respect I did not see many of my own Primera Iglesia Bautista pastors receive.

I never read a Dallas Willard book.

I did, however, find an interesting quote from his book *Knowing Christ Today: Why We Can Trust Spiritual Knowledge*: "Justice without love will never do justice to justice, nor will 'love' without justice ever do justice to love. Indeed, it will not be love at all."[1]

What does justice—with love—look like for Mexicans, Latinos, or Hispanics?

Justice is not when I don't get treated like "other Mexicans." Justice is when "other Mexicans" get treated like me.

Jesse Rincones is the executive director of Convención Bautista Hispana de Texas and a member of the Baptist Standard *board of directors. He returned to Alliance Baptist Church in Lubbock as pastor in 2021.*

---

[1]   Dallas Willard, *Knowing Christ Today: Why We Can Trust Spiritual Knowledge* (New York: HarperOne, 2009), 83.

49

Justice looks like God's will on earth as it is in heaven

Brenda Kirk

On the surface it seems a simple question. We all know what justice means to us. It's righting a wrong, fair and equitable treatment, right?

Lady Justice, portrayed in the United States as a blindfolded woman carrying a sword and a set of scales, is one of the most recognizable legal symbols. She symbolizes the fair and equal administration of the law, without corruption, greed, prejudice, or favor.

Unfortunately, our conscious and unconscious biases are not blind. Our sinful nature provokes us to justify greed and prejudice as well as privilege and favor. As a Christian, I have searched Scripture to help process my struggles with justice.

What justice doesn't look like

In 2003, my beloved sister—a decorated soldier—was brutally murdered in her apartment in my hometown in Oklahoma. Early on, I thought we would grieve the loss, law enforcement would investigate, and eventually there would be a day in court—an accounting of justice that did not happen.

By 2006, the pain was becoming bitterly rooted. I became aware I could not continue in the immensity of the grief, frustration, and anger that was consuming me. The next several years were spent searching for purpose, peace, and joy. I found and became very active in a women's ministry at my church.

One day, it became clear to me that at age nine, when I accepted Christ as my Savior and was baptized in a creek near the country church we attended, I had been forgiven. Now, my peace depended on my ability to forgive the unidentified murderer of my sister.

Finding peace and a new path

I wrestled with myself for months to find that peace. I remember the night it happened. While leading a group of women in a summer Bible study on Revelation, God spoke to me. I felt him strongly declaring his sovereignty to right the wrong.

Hence, my new path in life began, even if I did not fully recognize it at the time. It was one of those life-changing moments when I knew the God of heaven and earth was opening a door of renewal. In that moment, I was released from the strong, dark desire for vengeance.

I understood clearly that my pain and anger were directed not just to the man who committed my sister's murder, but to all those who had participated in the failures of the justice system. That betrayal opened my eyes to a fragmented system, which sought to protect those of status and favor.

Awakening to justice

In this current time, I also feel there is an awakening across our nation, a move of God. He is opening our eyes and ears, allowing us truly to understand the experiences, pains, and injustices hurting so many communities of color.

In his recent book, *One in Christ: Bridging Racial and Cultural Divides*, David D. Ireland provides an excellent look at how we are able to change. He explains that people can be changed in two ways: (1) when they are confronted with social and societal pressure or (2) when confronted with their own personal values and actions that do not align with their beliefs.[1] The second led to my moment of conversion.

True repentance comes from the inside out. The Holy Spirit convicts us of our sins, and we cry out in repentance, reverse our behavior, and come into alignment with God's desires.

---

[1]   David D. Ireland, *One in Christ: Bridging Racial and Cultural Divides* (Washington, D.C.: Regnery Faith, 2018).

What does justice look like for me? It looks this:

- John 3:16—"For God so loved the world."
- Micah 6:8—What God requires: "To act justly and to love mercy and to walk humbly with God."
- Matthew 6:10—The will of God done "on earth as it is in heaven."
- Revelation 7:9–12—"A great multitude that no one could count, from every nation, tribe, people and language, standing before the throne and before the Lamb."

Resources for learning about justice

If your church or study group desires to learn more, here are a few helpful resources:

- *One in Christ: Bridging Racial and Cultural Divides*, by David D. Ireland.
- *Multiethnic Conversations: An Eight-Week Journey toward Unity in Your Church*, by Mark DeYmaz and Oneya Fennell Okuwobi.
- *Welcome the Stranger: Justice, Compassion, & Truth in the Immigration Debate*, revised and expanded, by Matthew Soerens and Jenny Yang.
- *Thinking Biblically about Immigrants & Immigration Reform*, by the Evangelical Immigration Table.[2]
- GLOO and Barna church data on COVID-19 and the racial justice response.[3]

Brenda Kirk is the south-central regional mobilizer with the National Immigration Forum and the Evangelical Immigration Table.

---

[2] https://evangelicalimmigrationtable.com/thinkingbiblically.
[3] https://www.barna.com/research/a-call-to-action-part-2/.

50

Justice looks like sweeping up injustice

Ferrell Foster

When I was a boy, my mother made me sweep the concrete slab where she parked her car. For some reason, this made me angry. When I finished, I leaned the wooden broom against a chain-link fence bordering the slab with the express purpose that Mom might run over it and break it.

She did. And she spanked me for it even though she didn't know I had done it on purpose. In my young brain, that seemed unfair. She punished me for something she did; she drove the car that broke the broom.

Justice, however, is not just about obvious actions; it's about actions of intent. I got exactly what I deserved—punishment—for what I conspired for my mom to do—break the broom.

The set up

Intent matters. People sometimes do things to cause difficulty or pain for other people in a way that keeps the plotter from being punished and actually brings trouble onto the victim. Think of sibling rivalries where one kid provokes a brother or sister to fight back, and then the fighter gets in trouble.

Let's bring forward the metaphor of me, my mom, and the broom. Over the course of this nation's history, many white people in authority have set up legal brooms for Black people to break. And the system often didn't have my mom's wisdom. My mom saw through my ruse. When it comes to racial issues, we often do not see through the racial ruse.

Under this racial ruse, if a preacher in the 1960s led a group of Black people on a peaceful march through the city to have his people treated fairly, he and the other marchers are jailed for gathering unlawfully.

In other words, the white legal establishment set up a broom for the Black marchers to break. They set up the legal broom because they didn't want to clean up the injustices in their segregated society.

The racial ruse continued in the 1980s. The white establishment set up drug laws that would put more Blacks in jail by making the punishments for using "Black" drugs more severe than those commonly used by whites.

Whites and Blacks used drugs at about the same rates, but our prisons filled up with Black men—who were also tagged as felons, causing the loss of citizenship privileges.

It was another legal broom set up to be broken, and many of us white people didn't realize the legal system was so unjust. So we blamed Black people for breaking the broom we put there in the first place.

Effects of the set up

On and on, more brooms. Black people are pulled over by white law enforcement for all kinds of seemingly suspicious behavior, but really, their only "crime" is being Black. A Black man who gets questioned by police has a lifetime of experiences where he and people like him have been treated unjustly. It creates a situation fraught with danger as fear courses through the veins of those involved—whites afraid of Blacks, Blacks untrusting of cops.

Good cops can handle these tense situations. Frightened or racist cops reach for their guns much too quickly or resort to chokeholds or knees to the neck.

It only takes moments for a person in power to snuff out the life of another person. That is not justice; that is injustice—a "punishment" that far exceeds an alleged crime.

Justice and Jesus' followers

There is injustice in our streets, and this is especially important to Jesus' followers.

Matthew said Jesus fulfilled Isaiah's prophecy, "Here is my servant, whom I have chosen, my beloved, with whom my soul is well pleased."

Isaiah said God would put the divine Spirit upon this beloved one, and "he will proclaim justice to the Gentiles." This servant will "not break a bruised reed or quench a smoldering wick until he brings justice to victory" (Matthew 12:17–20).

Bringing justice leads to hope (v. 21).

Justice is a key requisite for hope. We pursue justice boldly, then, day in and day out, in honor of the calling of God as witnessed by Isaiah and Matthew and exemplified in Jesus.

My mom taught me so much when she punished me for setting her up to break the broom. True justice requires wisdom to think beyond what seems most obvious.

Put away the brooms of injustice, and there will be more justice. That clearly is a matter of deep Christian conviction.

Dr. Ferrell Foster is president and founder of Kortabocker LLC: Communications Built on Caring. He previously led care and communications with Prosper Waco, a nonprofit dedicated to education, health, and financial security from a perspective of addressing equity issues. Prior to that, he was director of ethics and justice for Texas Baptists. His articles have been published widely.

51

Justice looks like the church serving in the community

Jack Goodyear

In the preamble to the US Constitution, the authors state the document will "establish Justice" as a wish of "We the People." Looking throughout America's history and into America's present, we can deduce the accomplishment of that goal still is a work in progress.

A century ago, Langston Hughes wrote the following words in "Who but the Lord?":

> Now, I do not understand
> Why God don't protect a man
> From police brutality.
> Being poor and black,
> I've no weapon to strike back—
> So who but the Lord
> Can protect me?[1]

Sadly, these words still are relevant today.

As a nation, our treatment of Native Americans, Blacks, Hispanics, Asians, women, Catholics, refugees, immigrants, the poor, the oppressed, and many others has been unjust.

While the words of the Declaration of Independence and the US Constitution proclaim an intent of establishing justice and hope for an oppressed world, we have not always been faithful in practice to that virtue within our borders.

---

[1] Langston Hughes, "Who but the Lord?" https://www.poetryfoundation.org/poetrymagazine/browse?contentId=24641.

However, as a representative democracy, we are able to address these shortcomings and strive for a more perfect union.

Addressing justice justly

The privilege of addressing injustices is not without its difficulties, as Reinhold Niebuhr recognized in *Moral Man and Immoral Society*: "The question which confronts society is, how it can eliminate social injustice by methods which offer some fair opportunity of abolishing what is evil in our present society, without destroying what is worth preserving in it, and without running the risk of substituting new abuses and injustices in the place of those abolished."[2]

This sentiment was shared by James Madison, who eloquently discussed the difficulty in balancing freedom and faction in the *Federalist Paper* no. 10.[3] For a democracy to root out injustice without causing greater injustices has been a long-discussed and deliberated topic in this nation.

Too often, Christians find more comfort in remaining safely within the confines of our churches, rarely addressing complex issues of justice faced in our communities for fear of being perceived as too radical.

However, responsible Christian stewardship requires us to engage. As Martin Luther King Jr. said, "Injustice anywhere is a threat to justice everywhere."

No matter our country of residence, our calling as Christians must compel us to address the injustices in our societies.

The moral voice of religion

In *A Black Theology of Liberation*, James Cone wrote, "Theology can never be neutral or fail to take sides on issues related to the plight of the oppressed. For this reason, it can never engage in conversation about the nature of God without confronting those elements of human existence which threaten anyone's existence as a person. Whatever theology says about God and the world must arise out of

---

[2] Reinhold Niebuhr, *Moral Man and Immoral Society: A Study in Ethics and Politics* (New York: Charles' Scribner's Sons, 1938), 167.

[3] https://billofrightsinstitute.org/founding-documents/primary-source-documents/the-federalist-papers/federalist-papers-no-10/.

its sole reason for existence as a discipline: to assist the oppressed in their liberation."[4]

Cone continues, "Yahweh takes sides. . . . In the New Testament, Jesus is not for all, but for the oppressed, the poor and unwanted of society, and against oppressors. . . . God is active in human history, taking sides with the oppressed of the land."[5]

Although the church seemingly has waned in influence over the years, congregations still have prominent roles to play when addressing issues of injustice. The ability to organize people and to speak with moral authority on issues of injustice often has been a strength of the church.

Where would abolition be without the moral voice of religion? Where would civil rights and the nonviolent protest movement be without the moral authority found in the gospel?

Voice of the disadvantaged

Howard Thurman, in *Jesus and the Disinherited*, wrote, "In a society in which certain people or groups—by virtue of economic, social, or political power—have dead-weight advantages over others who are essentially without that kind of power, those who are thus disadvantaged know that they cannot fight back effectively, that they cannot protect themselves, and that they cannot demand protection from their persecutors."[6]

Injustice is prevalent in our society today.

Although the church competes in a cacophony of so many other voices in our society today, the church still can utilize its moral authority to drive toward justice by being the voice of the disadvantaged. The church has the ability to proclaim a narrative with moral persuasion that can strengthen the effectiveness of enacting justice in a community.

---

[4]   James Cone, *A Black Theology of Liberation*, 40th anniversary ed. (Maryknoll, N.Y.: Orbis, 2010), 4.

[5]   Cone, *Black Theology of Liberation*, 6.

[6]   Howard Thurman, *Jesus and the Disinherited*, 2022 ed. (Boston: Beacon, 2022), 27–28.

Justice looks like the church serving in the community, prophetically calling out those in power, sacrificially serving the oppressed, striving for the rights of others before themselves.

Our "more perfect" union, our establishment of justice in this land, will only be realized truly when the church embraces and lives out Micah 6:8, seeking to do justice, to love mercy, and to walk humbly with God.

Only then will those crying out for justice be able to share in the words of Langston Hughes when he wrote, "I'm still here!"

Jack Goodyear is the dean of the Cook School of Leadership and is a professor in political science at Dallas Baptist University. He holds a PhD in religion, politics, and society from Baylor University. His studies focused on the historical, philosophical, theological, and sociological interaction between religion and politics and the church and state, paying special attention to the impact of evangelicals in American politics and culture.

52

True justice looks like restoration and redemption

Kristin Houlé Cuellar

Justice looks like a second chance, even for those who have caused great harm.

Chris Young

On July 17, 2018, the State of Texas executed Chris Young despite the pleas of Mitesh Patel, who did not want the state to kill the man who murdered his father and sought desperately for state officials to listen to him.[1]

Young was executed despite the cries of his teenage daughters, who needed their father in their lives. He was executed despite his quest to be a productive member of society within and beyond the prison walls.

Young was sentenced to death in 2006 for the robbery and murder of a convenience store owner, Hash Patel, in San Antonio two years prior. He was twenty-one years old at the time of the crime and, like so many on death row, suffered terrible trauma as a child.

He was born to a teenage mother who moved the family multiple times and brought violent men into their lives. His own father was murdered when he was eight years old. Shortly thereafter, he turned to a street gang to fulfill his need for support and community.

By his own admission, Young had a lot of growing up to do when he arrived on death row. In the twelve years he spent there, he educated himself and became an artist.[2] He parented his daughter,

[1]   https://www.youtube.com/watch?v=u9RRZnzKvlo.
[2]   https://lawatthemargins.com/death-row-saved-my-life/.

Crishelle, through letters and her visits to the Polunsky Unit in Livingston.[3]

Through his active correspondence, Young also mentored troubled young people, including extended family members, to help them avoid the mistakes he made in his life.

The person the State of Texas executed was not the same man who killed Hash Patel. He deserved a second chance.

Billy Joe Wardlow

Texas carried out another senseless execution two years later, putting Billy Joe Wardlow to death on July 8, 2020.[4] He was the first person executed in Texas during the COVID-19 pandemic and the 570th person put to death by this state since 1982.

Like Young, Wardlow was treated by our state as nothing more than his worst act, an act he committed when he was only eighteen. In 1993, in rural Morris County, Wardlow panicked and killed Carl Cole during an attempt to steal Cole's truck. Wardlow and his girlfriend were desperate to run away to escape their abusive families.

The jury that sentenced Wardlow to death predicted he likely would be dangerous in the future, a determination required by Texas law to impose capital punishment. Nothing could be further from the truth.

During Wardlow's twenty-five years of incarceration on death row, he matured, was deeply introspective, and pursued his interest in a wide range of subjects. He was considered a kind and compassionate peacemaker who brought out the good in other men. And he truly was remorseful for taking Carl Cole's life.

Wardlow's jury did not have access to the information we have today about brain development, which shows our brains do not fully mature until we reach our early to mid-twenties. Provided with this scientific knowledge, two of his jurors came to believe Wardlow should serve a life sentence instead.

---

[3] https://lawatthemargins.com/i-dont-want-my-father-to-die/.

[4] https://theamericanscholar.org/this-man-should-not-be-executed/.

The jurors joined state legislators, juvenile justice advocates, neuroscience experts, and thousands of people nationwide who urged the courts and state officials to stop his execution, but to no avail.

Achieving true justice

The executions of Chris Young and Billy Wardlow did not make anyone safer or restore the families or communities they had hurt. Rather, ending their lives perpetuated a cycle of violence that left more victims in its wake.

Had Young and Wardlow been allowed to spend the rest of their natural lives in prison, they would have continued to have a positive impact on countless people. To me, they represent what justice *could* look like.

Instead of the retributive system of punishment we have today, true justice is restorative and redemptive. It is meted out fairly and proportionately. It recognizes an individual's capacity for change.

It addresses harm without inflicting more trauma. It promotes healing for victims. It means holding people accountable for their actions without denying their humanity.

To achieve justice, we must acknowledge our shared worth. We must recognize all of us are more than our worst act.

Kristin Houlé Cuellar is the executive director of the Texas Coalition to Abolish the Death Penalty, a statewide advocacy organization based in Austin. For more information, visit www.tcadp.org.

53

Justice looks like equity in the administration of justice

Michael Bell

I am a community activist who is a pastor, not the other way around.

Since age nineteen, I have been a member of several civil rights and community-interest organizations and have participated in or led protests, boycotts, sit-ins, and other nonviolent strategies in the pursuit of justice and equality for people of color, particularly African Americans.

Most recently, until the onset of the novel coronavirus, a community group of which I am a decades-long member was engaged in daily downtown protests. After we had been protesting for almost two years in the same location without any mentionable brush with local law enforcement, suddenly, without provocation or probable cause, a dozen police officers swooped in on those of us who were protesting and started writing citations for disorderly conduct, noise, and any other infraction they could conjure up. This happened almost every day for a month and a half.

We had been protesting peacefully within the parameters of city ordinances and state statutes without incident other than the routine harassment from those who had problems with African Americans observing their First Amendment right to "redress grievances."

Why were protesters who had not been cited even once for the twenty-three months prior receiving multiple citations *now*? And why did the writing of citations stop as abruptly as they started?

We discovered the timeline of the writing of citations was wed to the last month of a highly contested citywide election.

But we still had to hire attorneys and currently are bound up in litigation.

I refer to this because it illustrates the opposite of what justice looks like to me.

Inequitable administration

Justice looks like equity in the administration of justice in the criminal justice system, including policing, criminal prosecutions, trials, sentencing, felony disfranchisement, and incarceration.

Evidence of discriminatory abuse within the framework of the administration of justice is incontrovertible. Too often, the law enforcement apparatus acts outside the law to uphold the sociocultural-economic status quo, denying marginalized racial and ethnic groups equal protection by the courts and police.

The researchers Marc Mauer and Nazgol Ghandnoosh argue correctly, stating, "Persistent racial disparities in the justice system have been shown to harm both individuals in the system as well as their families and communities."[1]

What happens when an African American mother—Jackie Craig—calls the police because a white neighbor assaults her son, and the responding white officer, without provocation, insults and assaults her and her daughters?

Why is it OK for a peaceful demonstrator to be arrested without cause and then jailed and required to post bond?

Why is it not a problem with folks on "the other side of town" when the courts and police contravene the principles of justice and equal protection of the laws that should be the crux of any criminal justice system?

Mitigating racial disparities

In their 2014 study "Racial Disparities in Incarceration Increase Acceptance of Punitive Policies," Rebecca C. Hetey and Jennifer L. Eberhardt summarized, "We found that exposing [white] people to

---

[1] Marc Mauer and Nazgol Ghandnoosh, *Incorporating Racial Equity into Criminal Justice Reform* (Washington, D.C.: The Sentencing Project, 2014), 2.

extreme racial disparities in the prison population heightened their fear of crime and increased acceptance of the very policies that lead to those disparities."[2]

The truth is, "racial-disparity denial" exacerbates the systemic, structural, and institutional inequities that permeate every level of the *justice system*, from legislation to policing to sentencing.

How do we as a nation go about effectively addressing the anti-Black bias inherent in our institutions of justice?

Beyond conceptualizing relevant public policies—which frequently are ignored or dismissed—aimed at reducing racial and ethnic justice-system disparities, what are we (those of us who daily are impacted negatively by the racism implicit in our criminal justice system) to do?

Beginning to honestly answer this question is a good starting place toward mitigating the unwarranted racial disparities in the criminal justice system.

Dr. Michael Bell is pastor and resident theologian at Greater St. Stephen First Baptist Church in southeast Fort Worth. He also serves as facilitator of Unity in the Community Coalition, a consortium of more than twenty-five community groups and organizations.

---

[2] Rebecca C. Hetey and Jennifer L. Eberhardt, "Racial Disparities in Incarceration Increase Acceptance of Punitive Policies," *Psychological Science* 25, no. 10 (2014), https://journals.sagepub.com/doi/10.1177/0956797614540307.

54

For churches, justice should be in the core values
Jimmy Dorrell

After three lively breakfast conversations thirty years ago, five homeless men and women living under the overpass at Interstate 35 and N. 4th Street in Waco invited my wife and me to lead a Bible study with them.

On Sunday, September 20, 1992, a handful of us gathered below the roar of overhead traffic to read a chapter from Romans, sing a couple of songs, and discuss the issues they struggle with each day. They continued to invite us back and began to call our growing circle "Church Under the Bridge." One of the "panhandlers" changed his sign from "Work for Food" to "Come to Bible Study."

Over the next several months, deep friendships grew. Janet and I learned to listen genuinely to them, hear their stories of pain and rejection, and include them in the Sunday morning Bible studies as readers, pray-ers, and singers.

No matter how poorly they read, prayed, or sang, participation in the "church" laid the foundation for what would become a multicultural congregation of Black, white, and brown worshippers. They were poor and middle-class, ex-offenders, and college students and those with mental health issues and severe addictions.

As the circle grew wider, we realized God was up to something we were beginning to understand. To protect us from straying into the captivity of traditional church expectations, our group began to have conversations about our core values that should guide our future.

Our core values

The mutually agreed upon values were:

- Our call would be based on God's word, confirmed by the Holy Spirit and body of Christ.
- Our call was outwardly focused toward the unchurched who would rarely attend other churches.
- Our call was to the poor and marginalized.
- Biblical justice would be a guiding theme of our church.
- Our call was to be multicultural.
- Our call was to be interdenominational.
- We would de-emphasize attractive and expensive buildings.
- Discipleship would occur mostly through small groups.
- Our call was to be based on "life together."

These core values have proven significant, especially as the church grew. Expectations came out as statements and questions:

- "We need a building to keep us out of bad weather and the traffic noise above."
- "How do we handle the wide variety of doctrinal disparities, especially when some were clearly unbiblical?"
- "Do we let the prostitute read the Scripture or the alcoholic take a drink during the service or accept the outbursts of some of those with severe mental illness?"
- "How do we spend our relatively small budget?"
- "How do we respond to racial injustices in our own community?"

Injustices in our congregation

Perhaps even more challenging was what to do when we came face to face with injustices experienced by our congregation. Some experienced illegal arrests with no money for bond and unfair extended pretrial waits. Most of our working poor made minimum wage and could never break their poverty. Some of them worked three part-time jobs since employers refused to offer health insurance.

Affordable housing in our community was virtually filled; so many members of our church slept in cars or on the couches of friends. There were very few beds for those lower-income friends in addiction.

Ex-offenders struggled to find work because of past incarceration. Health care was nonexistent for those below some guidelines. Because Texas was forty-eighth out of fifty states in funds for the mentally ill, there were few caseworkers and providers to help them. The outdated public bus system took almost two hours to go anywhere, requiring workers to leave very early and get home late.

Responding to injustice here and beyond

The same year Church Under the Bridge began, a Christian foundation provided funds for us to create Mission Waco, Mission World. This nonprofit gave us the platform to address several of these formidable injustices.

We started a job-training program and worked with local employers to hire them. We created a Christian-based residential alcohol-and-drug home that far exceeds public recovery data. We built a fifty-six-bed homeless shelter called My Brother's Keeper and invited churches to lead evening devotions.

We found volunteer lawyers to give "advice" to our folks entangled in legal issues. We created the Meyer Center for Urban Ministries, staffed by social workers and mental health counselors and containing a free clinic and breakfast for the homeless.

We even created the Jubilee Food Market, a nonprofit grocery store, to provide healthy and affordable food for our food desert neighborhood.

Finally, based on our call to work "without borders," we now have a microloan program for women in Haiti, support for three hundred children to attend school, water-well drilling, some basic health care for a seminomadic Muslim group in India, and finances for a Baptist church in Mexico City that serves more than two hundred homeless each Sunday morning.

Church Under the Bridge helps fund several of these justice projects. In fact, almost one-half of our budget goes to empower them.

Our core values have continued to guide our direction and help us avoid the pitfalls of becoming apathetic to the world around us.

Jimmy Dorrell is the cofounder and president emeritus of Mission Waco, Mission World; a founder and director of the Texas Christian Community Development Network; pastor of Church Under the Bridge; and the author of four books.

55

Justice looks like wisdom: Abundance vs. scarcity
Garrett Vickrey

Justice looks like wisdom. Proverbs defined the good life as the establishment of justice, righteousness, and equity. We define the good life as accumulation of enough resources to keep us safe.

Throughout Scripture, we see wisdom is meant for the whole society, not just the individual. For any of us to flourish, it is wise that we enact justice that allows all of us to flourish. But do we believe this is an abundant world where all of us can flourish?

Abundance vs. scarcity

Walter Brueggemann argues the book of Exodus is about the contest between the liturgy of abundance and the myth of scarcity. He states, "The Pharaoh in Genesis 47, like Hitler after him, is afraid that there aren't enough good things to go around, he must try to have them all."[1]

Joseph is recruited to manage the monopoly. You know the rest of the story. A Pharaoh rose over Egypt who knew not Joseph. Once partners, the people of Israel became slaves.

The myth of scarcity is the greatest obstacle to justice in our time and Joseph's.

When justice and equity were forfeited for the sake of profit, the prophets protested. Israel became like any other nation. They inverted the promises of the Abrahamic covenant. Instead of being

---

[1] Walter Brueggemann, "The Liturgy of Abundance, the Myth of Scarcity," *Christianity Today*, March 24–31, 1999, https://www.religion-online.org/article/the-liturgy-of-abundance-the-myth-of-scarcity/.

blessed to be a blessing, they cursed their enemies, hoarded their resources, and lost their sense of vocation.

Today, Pharaoh's heirs and surrogates justify selfishness through myth making—aka "fake news"—and stereotyping that turns neighbor against neighbor. For instance, there is the myth of the welfare queen or lazy poor people. We justify hoarding resources by saying if "they"—and you know who *they* are—worked hard enough, they could break out of the cycle of poverty.

But it's expensive to be poor. If you miss a bill, you get fined. If you get a loan, you have to pay back higher interest. If you don't have enough money in the bank, you are charged monthly fees. If you ever overdraft your account because your paycheck doesn't hit the bank at just the right time, then you are penalized with more fees. The system doesn't want you out of the cycle.

The myth of scarcity turns partners into rivals. We desacralize the poor and those we deem unworthy of justice, hollowing out the hallowed image of God in them so we can dehumanize and justify our selfishness.

Choosing between the two

Proverbs 18:1–2 implores us, "He who isolates himself pursues his desires; he disdains all competence. The fool does not desire understanding, but only to air his thoughts."

During the past eighteen months, the foolishness of isolationism has been laid bare. Now, it seems vaccine hesitancy has fed the fires of a fourth COVID surge just in time for the start of a new school year.

The poet John Donne speaks prophetically, "No man is an island . . . and therefore never send to know for whom the bell tolls; it tolls for thee."[2]

We clearly see the importance of paid sick leave for essential workers who feel pressure to go to work even though they have COVID symptoms because if they miss a paycheck, they will face

---

[2] John Donne, "For Whom the Bell Tolls," https://web.cs.dal.ca/~johnston/poetry/island.html.

eviction. Health care for all is looking more and more like wisdom in a world as small as ours.

Yet we will not know wisdom until we stop giving fools platforms and clicking "like" on lies. Justice looks like wisdom. Wisdom builds up communities rather than stoking the fires of culture wars with misinformation.

The myth of scarcity obstructs any effort to work for justice. It is cloaked as righteous fear and speaks in the rhetoric of "whataboutism": "What about the looters?" "What about the violence in the streets?" "What about issue X that's never mentioned?"

The obstacles are within each of us. Police enforce my prejudice. Politicians enact public policy that assuages my fears. Preachers like me preach to keep people in pews.

And the doubts creep as Pharaoh's fears become our own. Do I have enough to be safe? Will there be enough for me? The contest of Exodus continues.

We must choose. Do we believe in Pharaoh's economy or the God who provides? There is only one wise choice.

Garrett Vickrey is the senior pastor of Woodland Baptist Church in San Antonio. He is a graduate of Baylor University and the Wake Forest University School of Divinity.

56

Justice looks like the cross
Rolando D. Aguirre

"This is not fair." These are my children's words when they believe my wife and I have not been fair in our parenting when we discipline them. This expression is heard constantly and articulated by different people across generations and particularly in our day. Why? Because this phrase is connected intrinsically to our sense of justice.

Our families, congregations, cities, and nation constantly are conflicted and polarized regarding this controversial topic.

Justice in its simplest terms means "to set things right."

Yet, how do we know what is right? Who defines *right*? Is it society at large or the culture we live in? Is there a moral law we inherently know to follow?

In an attempt to respond to what justice looks like, I have to start by stating true justice flows from God's heart and character.

Justice flows from God

God's love and holiness revolve around his justice. In his love, God does not want to repay us based on what we deserve, but in his justice, he has to discipline us lovingly.

A gripping example of this often is seen in the Old Testament when Yahweh addresses issues of sin and injustice. These judgments are individual and corporate in scope.

As Christ followers, the answer to what justice looks like is clear. Jesus is our standard of righteousness. Jesus Christ lived a perfect and sinless life, died a sacrificial death, and rose again to make right that which was wrong. It is because of Jesus and his work on the cross that we can be declared just and made right with a holy God.

Our sense of justice is imparted to us by our Creator, God. He is loving, kind, and merciful, and he is also righteous, holy, and just. He defines and sets the standard for justice.

We hear "God is love and holy" more often than we hear "God is just." We may readily agree God sets the standard for love and holiness, but do we understand he also sets the standard for justice?

Jesus calls followers to justice

As we look at the life of Jesus and the mandate given throughout Scripture, it is clear Christ followers are called to "do justice." We are called to take action and confront evil, to care for the vulnerable, and to make right that which is wrong. This mandate is not new. It is not a cultural fad or simply a trend in today's society.

Jesus himself pursued justice. Pursuing biblical justice means we follow God's way to make right that which is wrong, and we look to Scripture to define what is "right."

In the New Testament, Jesus also demonstrates a beautiful example for us to follow as one who cared for the outcast and reached out with compassion to help those most often overlooked. He physically and spiritually rescued those in need. The healing of the leper in Matthew 8 and caring for the woman caught in adultery in John 8 are just two examples.

The prophet Isaiah declared, "Learn to do good; seek justice, correct oppression; bring justice to the fatherless, and plead the widow's cause" (Isaiah 1:17).

The foundational verse for many social justice–related matters expressly communicates, "He has told you, O man, what is good; and what does the Lord require of you but to do justice, and to love kindness, and to walk humbly with your God?" (Micah 6:8).

"Justice is the cross"

Rev. Samuel Rodriguez stated that in the kingdom of God, "justice is the cross." No other symbol incorporates more passion and promise than the cross. Jesus said, "Carry your cross daily and follow me."

The cross has both a vertical and horizontal dimension. Vertically, we remain connected to God, his kingdom, and eternal life, a wonderful spiritual truth with divine principles and glory. Horizontally—to our left and to our right—we are surrounded by our community, relationships, family, culture, and society.

Just like the cross is vertical and horizontal, so is redemption and relationship. It is both covenant and community, both kingdom and society that beautifully reflect righteousness and justice.

Salvation and transformation

Only God can save and transform a person into his likeness and image. It is where John 3:16 and Matthew 25 merge. It typifies the qualities of both a Billy Graham and a Martin Luther King Jr.

Justice is the blending of both believing prayer and arising to act justly. It is biblical faith walking in shoe leather, doing what is right and embracing social justice while honoring the teaching of Scripture. It is faith fleshed out into good works, where loving God with a pure heart leads to loving those around us in a just and right way.

Why do we honor the oppressed, the downtrodden, the underprivileged? Because more than two thousand years ago, the eternal God-man came and showed us the way to live daily—loving God, loving others, and doing what is right and just. That is what justice looks like for his great name's sake.

Dr. Rolando D. Aguirre is the associate pastor of teaching and Spanish language ministries at Park Cities Baptist Church in Dallas.

57

What justice looks like for families of suspects and defendants

Christine Abel Nix

The mother of a capital-murder defendant telephoned months after the trial requesting assistance on an unrelated matter.

During the trial, the mother and other family members understandably were distant from law enforcement officers. At times, the family members were uncomfortable and maintained a self-imposed distance. The mother stated she did not know who she could ask for help.

I often have thought about this interaction and the fate of families whose loved one was suspected of or tried for a crime that shocked the moral and legal conscience.

Whether a person is on trial for or found guilty of killing someone during the commission of a crime, family members of the defendant can be condemned as guilty by association. I label this group unnamed victims of crime, or UVC.

Treatment of unnamed victims of crime

There is no category for UVCs in academic research. UVCs are siloed and set aside until needed for court testimony or a documentary.

It is not uncommon for these families to receive direct and veiled threats due to their loved one's criminal action(s). Social media is a breeding ground for untoward comments and rants aimed at innocent family members, often for the sole purpose of gaining "likes" and reposts.

I am surprised at the negativity expressed by people who profess to be steadfast in their faith but condemn UVCs for a family member's criminal behavior.

Recently, a professing Christian stated the closest relative of a suspect—who died during an altercation with police—should not receive the same consideration and respect at the funeral as other crime victims. This person also believed a negatively written communication to the immediate surviving family member was appropriate.

Grace and mercy for UVCs

Once a UVC situation occurs, it presents a unique challenge and opportunity for Christians in a community upended by a heinous crime.

Grace and mercy are not the responsibility of the criminal justice system. With the real and perceived gap between UVCs and the community, Christians must be examples of compassionate understanding. Doing so helps to minimize potential delinquency and adult antisocial behaviors resulting from marginalization due to a family member's criminal actions.

How often does the community or members of a congregation reach out and offer heartfelt condolences to UVCs?

Recently, a suspect was shot and killed after wounding a police officer and a civilian. An elected official sent well-wishes to the injured and condolences to the family of the suspect. The elected official was requested to explain offering condolences to the family of the deceased suspect. The official said the UVC lost a loved one, good or bad, and questioned how and why society avidly objects to showing sympathy for the loss of a family member regardless of the situation.

Christians are obligated to care for UVCs

As Christians, we cannot wait for directives or imperatives from academic research or criminal justice–policy implementations to determine the potential adverse outcomes of the lack of support for UVCs. Scripture is our directive. Proverbs 10:12 states, "Hatred stirs up strife, but love covers all sins."

As members of the family of Christ, we forego an opportunity to witness to, welcome, and love these unnamed victims of crime if we hold them guilty for the actions of a family member.

As we do with crime victims, we should follow the model of eliminating questions of "why" or "why didn't you?" Instead, we should inquire what we can do or how we can help UVCs move forward. How can we, as Christians, meet the needs of this underserved population?

As Christians, we should be available and willing helpers while simultaneously standing as a frontline of defense for these families.

Isaiah's commission always has resonated with me. "Then I heard the voice of the Lord saying, 'Whom shall I send, and who will go for us?' And I said, 'Here am I. Send me'" (Isaiah 6:8).

I was the primary investigator on the capital-murder investigation mentioned at the beginning of this article. That call was instrumental in changing my perception of unnamed victims of crime and their alienation within the community.

What might change your perception of them?

Dr. Christine Abel Nix is a retired Texas law enforcement officer and currently serves as an associate professor of criminal justice.

58

Justice looks like what Scripture tells us

Stephen Reeves

Scripture tells us what justice looks like.
Justice looks like this:

- Water flowing down (Amos 5).
- An ear inclined toward the orphan and the oppressed (Psalm 10).
- No wrong or violence to the alien, the orphan, or the widow (Jeremiah 22).
- Food to the hungry (Psalm 149).
- Stability in the land (Proverbs 29).
- Doing good, rescuing the oppressed, defending the orphan, and pleading for the widow (Isaiah 1).
- Delivery from the hand of the oppressor by anyone who has been robbed (Jeremiah 21).
- Joy to the righteous, but dismay to evil doers (Proverbs 29).
- What we're required to do (Micah 6).
- Zacchaeus paying back four times what he stole from others (Luke 19).
- Doing unto "the least of these" as we would do unto Christ himself (Matthew 25).
- Loving your neighbor as yourself (Leviticus 19:18; Mark 12:31–33; Matthew 19:19; 22:39; Luke 10:27; Romans 13:9; Galatians 5:14; James 2:8).

These powerful images should be formative. They should shape not only our personal morality but also our public engagement. How might we exercise a Christian citizenship that promotes and fulfills this biblical view of justice?

Justice vs. injustice

Justice looks like hospitality and welcoming the stranger. Injustice looks like separating families, rejecting asylum seekers, refusing refugees, and locking kids in cages. Injustice allows forces of white Christian nationalism to influence policy.

Justice looks like fairness. Injustice looks like record-low interest rates for the wealthy while the financially vulnerable and desperate are charged more than 400 percent APR on payday and auto title loans.[1]

Justice looks like generosity. Injustice looks like one in three households with children unable to afford food, housing, or utilities at least once from 2014 to 2016.[2]

Justice looks like daily bread. Injustice looks like hunger rates for Black and Latino families twice that of white families.[3]

Justice looks like equality. Injustice looks like the top three richest Americans owning more wealth than the bottom half of all Americans.[4] Injustice looks like the typical white family owning nearly ten times the wealth of a typical Black family.[5]

Justice looks like opportunity. Injustice looks like overwhelmingly white school districts receiving $23 billion more in state and local funding than predominantly nonwhite schools serving the

---

[1] https://www.texasappleseed.org/sites/default/files/Texas2018.pdf.

[2] https://www.cbpp.org/research/poverty-and-inequality/widespread -economic-insecurity-pre-pandemic-shows-need-for-strong.

[3] https://frac.org/foodinsufficiencycovid19.

[4] https://inequality.org/wp-content/uploads/2017/11/BILLIONAIRE -BONANZA-2017-Embargoed.pdf.

[5] https://www.brookings.edu/blog/up-front/2020/02/27/examining -the-black-white-wealth-gap/.

same number of students,[6] and Black students attending schools just as segregated now as in the 1960s and '70s.[7]

Justice looks like freedom. Injustice looks like mass incarceration and the United States having the highest incarceration rate in the world, where Black Americans are incarcerated at a rate more than five times higher than whites.[8] Injustice looks like a bail system where the poor remain in jail before they're ever convicted of a crime just because they are poor.[9]

Justice looks like a sustainable relationship with God's creation and natural resources. Injustice looks like those least responsible for carbon dioxide emissions being most impacted by climate change.[10]

Justice looks like a functional democracy that affirms the equality and God-given dignity of every voter. Injustice looks like restricting access to the ballot by reduced early voting, improper purges of electoral rolls, closing polling places, voters waiting in line all day to cast a ballot, and 6.1 million Americans being barred from voting due to felony disenfranchisement.[11] Injustice looks like political districts so gerrymandered they reduce the influence of communities and ensure reelection of incumbents.

Justice looks like a country where the likelihood of a family thriving cannot be predicted by the color of their skin. Injustice looks like health care systems that repeatedly fail our Black and Latino

[6] https://www.washingtonpost.com/local/education/report-finds-23-billion-racial-funding-gap-for-schools/2019/02/25/d562b704-3915-11e9-a06c-3ec8ed509d15_story.html.

[7] https://equitablegrowth.org/research-paper/u-s-school-segregation-in-the-21st-century/.

[8] https://www.statista.com/statistics/262962/countries-with-the-most-prisoners-per-100-000-inhabitants/; https://www.sentencingproject.org/publications/color-of-justice-racial-and-ethnic-disparity-in-state-prisons/.

[9] http://cjpp.law.harvard.edu/assets/BailReform_WEB.pdf.

[10] https://www.nytimes.com/2020/07/30/climate/bangladesh-floods.html.

[11] https://www.sentencingproject.org/publications/felony-disenfranchisement-a-primer/.

neighbors, including in infant and maternal mortality rates,[12] death from diabetes,[13] and rates of being uninsured.[14]

Justice looks like empathy. Injustice refuses to see from another's perspective, to acknowledge their experience is different from ours, or to believe their testimony.

Seeing and seeking justice

Justice looks like striving to live up to our American ideal that all are created equal. Justice looks like those doing well themselves working for a better future for neighbors who struggle.

We cannot see justice when we are motivated by anger and fear. To see justice, we must raise our gaze above the partisanship and cynicism that limits our vision. We cannot see justice with a scarcity mindset that refuses to embrace God's abundance. To see justice, we must engage our prophetic imagination that envisions God's kingdom here on earth as it is in heaven.

Justice cannot prevail when we perpetuate unjust systems because they protect our own power and privilege. Justice cannot be the goal of only one political party or one "type" of Christian.

If we're going to achieve liberty and justice for all, it will take us all. Every American, and certainly every follower of Christ, should be committed to seeking justice; it's what we're called to do. Justice looks like the promise of equality finally fulfilled instead of a dream too long deferred.

Stephen Reeves serves as executive director of Fellowship Southwest and as director of advocacy for the Cooperative Baptist Fellowship. A native of Austin, he is the former director of public policy for the Texas Baptist Christian Life Commission, is a member of the State Bar of Texas, and a graduate of the University of Texas at Austin and Texas Tech School of Law.

[12] https://www.cdc.gov/reproductivehealth/maternalinfanthealth/infantmortality.htm; https://www.cdc.gov/reproductivehealth/maternal-mortality/disparities-pregnancy-related-deaths/infographic.html.

[13] https://www.cdc.gov/nchs/data/hus/2016/017.pdf.

[14] https://www.kff.org/racial-equity-and-health-policy/issue-brief/eliminating-racialethnic-disparities-in-health-care-what/.

59

Justice looks like Onesimus, the bishop of Ephesus

Pastor Samuel James Doyle

The church should be the first institution Christians should consider to examine what justice looks like.

Before advocating for it in the world, we should examine the quality of it in our own community and seek to understand what God's view of justice is.

In God's word we will discover it, with one another we should practice it, and before the world we should advocate for it.

For me, the most helpful place to see this justice practiced is in the life of Onesimus, the bishop of Ephesus.

Onesimus' story

We first read of Onesimus in Paul's prison letters Philemon and Colossians. His story begins in the house of Philemon, a slaveholding house-church leader and the recipient of the letter that bears his name.

Paul wrote to Philemon, appealing on behalf of Onesimus. His implicit request advocated for Onesimus' full release. His explicit request appealed for Onesimus' warm reception as a "beloved brother."

After all, it was Onesimus who would return to Colossae with letters from Paul to the church there. He would deliver the first letter to the church at Colossae, relaying to them—along with Tychicus—Paul's condition of well-being and comforting the Colossians' hearts.

In Colossians 4:9, Paul calls Onesimus a "faithful and beloved brother," clearly indicating his new status as a minister and church leader. Imagine, therefore, how emotionally heavy it must have been for Onesimus to deliver this second letter to the man who would only see him as a slave—even still, his property.

Paul's admonishment to Philemon is clear. Onesimus is "no longer a slave," he is your "brother beloved." Philemon, therefore, is instructed to receive Onesimus as if he were receiving Paul.

Onesimus is now *beloved*: created in Christ for good works prepared for him before the foundation of the world. He is *beloved*: born through the blood, claimed by grace, redeemed by mercy, lifted by love, captured by hope, and astounded by glory.

He is *beloved*: purchased by God, loved by Paul, and—with the transforming, barrier-breaking power of the gospel—he will be received by Philemon as his brother, never again his slave.

Paul's ask

Although Paul never comes out and says, "Release Onesimus and let him come back to Rome with me so he can preach the gospel full-time," this is clearly what he is asking for.

After all, emancipation is the only realistic way Philemon ever could regard Onesimus as "no longer a slave." If he is "no longer a slave," it has to follow he is not obligated to remain with Philemon because he cannot simultaneously be Philemon's brother *and* his slave.

In fact, the heavy ethical implications of the gospel leave absolutely no room for any Christian ever to lord over another because the concept of supremacy is completely inconsistent with the grace of Christ's cross, which renders everyone equal.

The rest of the story

The lives of Onesimus and Philemon do not end with the biblical account. According to church tradition, Philemon went on to be the bishop of Colossae, Onesimus went on to be the bishop of Ephesus, and both men were martyred during the reign of Nero.

If this is true, then the slave owner and the slave would have abandoned their worldly titles and received one another as beloved brothers, serving together, leading together, and ultimately dying together.

Sadly, modern scholarship doubts these events. In fact, a great deal of the commentary regarding Philemon is clouded by a fog of speculation, such as theories that Onesimus robbed Philemon and that Paul was writing to assure him Onesimus would be a good slave if allowed to return. For the most part, however, these speculations are mere eisegetical products of Western sensitivities.

The pain and loss Paul describes in verse 18 could be explained sufficiently by Onesimus' escape. More so, receiving Onesimus back as a "good slave" completely ignores Paul's crystal-clear language of "no longer a slave."

Concerning their doubt that Onesimus the slave became Onesimus the bishop, they cite the commonness of his name. However, there is only *one* Onesimus from Colossae—near Ephesus—who is listed among Paul's ministry converts and colleagues.

It therefore makes sense that he is the one who became bishop of Ephesus. The only reason such a claim is unacceptable to modern scholarship is that they suffer from eyes that refuse to see.

Seeing anew

It appears, therefore, that for the twenty-first-century Western reader, the book of Philemon helps the church see why our vision of justice is so cloudy. We have a hermeneutic that simply refuses to see slaves and slaveholders giving up their worldly barriers for the sake of their fraternal bond in Christ.

We have been conditioned to see a gospel that keeps slaves as slaves and teaches slave owners how to be benevolent masters. In courageous abandon of our often polarized lenses, what if we began to see the gospel for what it truly does for us: breaking down every single barrier that hinders us from being family in Jesus—living together, serving together, witnessing together, praying together, dying together, overcoming together, and reigning with Christ in glory forever together. This is kingdom justice.

From the balconies of heaven, Philemon and Onesimus beseech us to let gospel love destroy every cultural, institutional, and systemic barrier that keeps us from being family so God's justice can be seen in the world when they look at the church.

Rev. Samuel James Doyle is a husband, father, brother, uncle, and follower of Jesus Christ. He and his wife Erika, along with their two daughters, reside in Waco, where he currently serves as the senior pastor of the Greater New Light Missionary Baptist Church.

60

Justice looks like leaning into grief

Ali Corona

> The grief of what it means to be Black in this country founded on white supremacist ideals and being a witness to mass Black death, compounded due to a highly contagious virus we still don't fully understand and state violence at the hands of police, is beyond what many of us could've expected to weather in our lifetime.
> —Nneka Okona[1]

Grief expresses itself in many different ways. Some people cry; others get angry. Some deflect uncomfortable feelings of vulnerability with busy work or humor.

Similarly, it is difficult to respond well to another person's grief. Far too often, and in the absence of knowing what to do with another person's suffering, we are content with indifference. We easily can convince ourselves the grieving person—or people—would rather be alone. We avoid getting involved with a "not-my-fight, not-my-problem" mentality.

Is our response to such great mourning to be squeamish and back away?

Perhaps we pick apart the things a person says in their grief until there's nothing left to take seriously. Perhaps witnessing another person's mourning makes us uncomfortable, especially when we are complicit in the system that oppresses.

[1] Nneka Okona, "We're in a New Age of Black Grief," *Well+Good*, July 27, 2020, https://www.wellandgood.com/new-age-black-grief-pandemic/.

What is the best way to respond to an individual's grief? How do we respond to collective grief?

The process is messy and uncomfortable, but helping professionals and pastors can attest to this truth: leaning in toward someone who is suffering is a gift.

It is a sacred thing to be let into another person's pain. Perhaps, culturally speaking, we don't know what to do with it. But it is holy.

Gaslighting

As a therapist, a common response I see to grief is a practice called gaslighting. Gaslighting is a manipulative tactic people who are abusive use to control another person. The person in power not only systematically lies but makes the vulnerable person feel crazy for questioning them.

They will shift blame for their abuse to the victim instead of taking responsibility. This, in turn, causes victims not to trust themselves, to feel responsible for the suffering, and, often, to apologize to the abuser.

Healing from psychological manipulation takes time, often years and decades. Gaslighting is beyond insensitive. It's cruel.

Watching the nation's events unfold over the last many months, I've been thinking a lot about gaslighting. It's hard to bear witness to ways in which white evangelicals have behaved with indifference to the suffering of Black people and people of color in America. It's been centuries.

It has been painful to see the ways gaslighting shows up to silence people our societies have oppressed for years.

I think about the pure strength it takes each time a client in my office chooses to believe truth when faced with years of being lied to and belittled. I can't help but think about this when I read and listen to Black voices and people of color who are sharing their experiences willingly after the death of Breonna Taylor, George Floyd, Ahmaud Arbery, and so many more.

People are mourning the sin and abuse of racism on a national scale.

Lean in and listen

There is so much that encompasses justice and action. I confess I am no expert. But one clear aspect is for white people to lean in toward the pain, loss, and frustrations of many in Black communities and communities of color.

This is the time to listen humbly and appreciate the holiness of these moments, the privilege it is to be let into someone's pain and suffering and take it seriously.

Justice does not end with privileged people listening, but it does begin with it.

I never will forget the first time I held a counseling session—the smell of coffee wafting in the air, tissues within reach, framed encouragements on the wall to warm the room, and most importantly, the brave woman sitting before me. She cried as she shared her story of abuse.

Her story was heart-wrenching and grave, and I remember becoming even more aware of the gravity of the situation. There was stillness in the air between us. I was nervous and deeply grateful she let me into her world. I still feel that way when I think of her.

In her book *Be the Bridge*, Latasha Morrison encourages Christians to empathize and mourn. "Acknowledgement should lead us toward lament, toward seeking mercy, toward a collective conviction that we can and must do better," she writes.[2]

Perhaps we don't know where grief belongs in our world. But Jesus did. The kingdom of heaven is for those who mourn.

Ali Corona is a licensed clinical social worker (LCSW) in Marble Falls. She has experience working with clients dealing with mental illness, sexual assault, domestic violence, and other forms of trauma. Ali attends First Baptist Church of Marble Falls with her husband, Jordan, and sons.

[2] Latasha Morrison, *Be the Bridge: Pursuing God's Heart for Racial Reconciliation* (New York: WaterBrook, 2019), 46.

61

Justice for mental illness is personal and systemic
Jessie Higgins

While working toward my master's degree in counseling, I imagined I'd be a very wise, very successful couples therapist who would arbitrate discussions about how one should fold the socks and which one should put the kids to bed, all while deftly addressing underlying hurts of childhood and wounds of adult life.

When I graduated at the fresh age of twenty-five and almost immediately moved to a city where I had zero professional connections, I was offered not the private practice job of my dreams but an entry-level position at the county's mental health agency.

I was lucky enough to find myself on a team serving the clients with the most severe mental health struggles. Although the work was different, my calling to couples counseling led me to see not only how complex family life can be but also how the struggle of mental health becomes compounded through the injustices of public health, poverty, isolation, and loneliness.

As I see it, justice is a calling—something innate within each of us, a key part of how God made us in his own image.

Justice is righting the wrong, mending the fracture, healing the ache. Justice is a promise to us from God that God is working for our good and gives us the same work ethic.

Mental wellness and justice
I quickly realized the folks I was working with—people with severe diagnoses and intense battles with drug and alcohol use—needed

someone to get down in the trenches and join them in the fight for justice.

You may not think of the mental-wellness journey as a "fight for justice," but for those who are experiencing a persistent mental illness combined with unrelenting poverty, every day can be a fight.

My clients were trying to keep track of complicated medication regimens and working through past traumas. At the same time, they were trying to survive in a bureaucratic system. The system had, among other things, given an annual increase of monthly Supplemental Security Income disability payments of two dollars but lowered monthly Supplemental Nutrition Assistance Program payments by two dollars.

Where was the justice? Where was even the potential for justice?

In a system so inherently broken by political maneuvering, unfounded fears fueled by stigma, and outsider-led policy making, there currently is little opportunity for healing or restoration.

Individual ways to fight for justice

To help change this current situation, individuals can fight for justice on a deeply personal level. You can make eye contact and small talk with people you usually would avoid in public places. You can talk about your own experiences with therapy and check in on friends going through difficult times.

Congregations and community groups can fight for justice on a bigger scale. They can pay for mental health services for members who cannot afford them. They can talk about depression, anxiety, paranoia, and other "symptoms" from the pulpit. They can institute trauma-informed care practices starting in children and youth ministries and radiating out from there.

Some of these ideas probably seem intuitive and may be steps you already are taking. However, these steps must be coupled with an even bigger response.

Justice is personal, and it also is systemic.

Addressing the system

In Matthew 25:32, the Son of Man addresses "all the nations" and names the "righteous" as those who took care of "the least of these."

To continue the fight for justice, we must address systemic—statewide and nationwide—issues.

There must be social workers and counselors in all schools. There must be a way to access mental health care even without private health insurance. There must be available interventions before a person is considering suicide as the only option.

Oftentimes, we confuse the political with the partisan. These issues certainly can have political solutions, but they do not need to be partisan.

Known by our love

Whenever I need a reminder of my calling, I remember doing a routine assessment with a client one day. I asked him if he believed in God. He answered, "I believe in God, but I know he doesn't care about me."

I take Jesus' words in John 13:35 very seriously: "By this everyone will know that you are my disciples, if you love one another." So it felt like a gut punch to hear his answer.

I believe in a God who cares for all so deeply that he sent his beloved Son to die for us. We are to show God's love in everything—from our personal interactions to working for meaningful policy and legislative change—always fighting for a society that cherishes one another, no matter who they are.

Jessie Higgins lives in San Antonio with her husband and cat. She is the Chief Mental Health Officer for the city of San Antonio and attends Trinity Baptist Church.

62

Justice is a constant gut check

Felisi Sorgwe

Injustice in society is not a new phenomenon. The Bible has a lot to say about justice, often linking the twin traits of righteousness and justice.

Righteousness is being upright in your vertical, one-on-one relationship with God, while justice is dealing with other human beings in a loving, fair, considerate, and equitable manner.

These two themes were reflected in our Lord's answer to the lawyer who tested him by asking what the greatest commandment in the law was.

Our Lord quoted from Deuteronomy 6:5—"You shall love the Lord your God with all your heart, with all your soul, and with all your mind"—and said this was the greatest and the first commandment.

He added a second commandment like the first, quoting from Leviticus 19:18—"You shall love your neighbor as yourself."

Our Lord then concluded, "On these two commandments hang all the law and the prophets" (Matthew 22:40).

What our Lord called the first and greatest commandment is a definition of righteousness, while what he called the second-to-greatest commandment leads to justice. James would refer to the second of these commandments as "the royal law" (James 2:8).

Injustice in the eighth century

Injustice seems to rear its ugly head more in times of prosperity. More affluent societies have the tendency to accept injustice—oppression—more readily as a way of life.

In the divided kingdom of Israel, King Uzziah of Judah and King Jeroboam II of Israel, in the eighth century BC, led the two kingdoms into a prosperous era. As it often happens, the prosperity functioned to widen the gap between the haves and the have-nots and to bring about the oppression of the have-nots by the haves.

God used the eighth-century prophets to condemn the injustice in no uncertain terms. God's prophets always spoke for the oppressed, giving a voice to the voiceless, never to sanction the oppressor's acts or statements.

Amos

Amos called out the oppressors of Israel for oppressing the poor and crushing the needy (Amos 4:1); for "afflicting the just and taking bribes" (Amos 5:12); for "diverting the poor from justice at the gate" (Amos 5:12); and for "making the ephah small and the shekel large, falsifying the scales by deceit, that [they] may buy the poor for silver, and the needy for a pair of sandals—even sell the bad wheat" (Amos 8:5–6).

The haves were dubiously finding ways to cheat the poor when they were buying items from them, as well as when they were selling anything to them. Amos, therefore, would cry out, "But let justice run down like water, and righteousness like a mighty stream" (Amos 5:24).

Isaiah

Isaiah pointed out that the plunder of the poor was in the houses of the oppressors, who were crushing God's people and "grinding the faces of the poor" (Isaiah 3:14–15). Isaiah also blamed the oppressors for justifying the wicked for a bribe and taking away justice from the righteous man (Isaiah 5:23).

Micah

Micah pronounced woe on the evildoers devising iniquity on their beds and acting out the plans in broad daylight "because it is in the power of their hand" (Micah 2:1).

The evildoers would "covet fields and take them by violence, also houses, and seize them" (Micah 2:2), thus demonstrating they did not know justice, hated what was good, and loved what was evil (Micah 3:1–2).

Micah would go on to give us what often is referred to as "the golden rule of the Old Testament," saying God clearly had shown the people what was good. "He has shown you, O man, what is good; And what does the Lord require of you but to do justly, to love mercy, and to walk humbly with your God?" (Micah 6:8).

Micah's declaration indeed would be partly restated in "the golden rule" of our Lord. "Therefore, whatever you want men to do to you, do also to them, for this is the Law and the Prophets" (Matthew 7:12).

Injustice in conflict with the gospel

In our Lord's parable of the unjust judge, the unjust judge had no fear of God and no regard for man (Luke 18:1–8). It is people like the unjust judge who thrive on injustice. It is a contradiction in terms to embrace injustice on one hand and to claim to be a proclaimer or an adherent of the gospel of Jesus Christ on the other.

Injustice can manifest itself in meting out unequal justice or withholding or delaying due justice. The class, race, or affiliation of the person never should be the determining factor in considering justice.

The late Congressman John Lewis challenged all of us, "If something is not right, not just, say something, do something."

If you cannot say something to condemn wrongdoing, at least do not rationalize it, let alone say something in approval of the act or statement.

It is not that hard to detect injustice, but you are faced with an unavoidable gut-check question in each situation. Will you condemn it, turn a blind eye to it, rationalize it, approve of it, or engage in it?

Dr. Felisi Sorgwe is associate professor of theology at Houston Christian University and pastor of Maranatha International Church in Houston.

63

Justice looks like "teaching, modeling, and equipping"

Bobby Hall

God's people have a long history of injustice and unrighteousness. As recorded in the book of Numbers, the Israelites made a career of crying out to God while in need, taking his provision, and humbling themselves before him . . . until they once again were unsatisfied. Throughout history, we repeat this same pattern over and over and over again.

Remember the sordid story of King David's affair with Bathsheba in 1 Samuel 11. Bathsheba became pregnant, and David had her husband, Uriah the Hittite, sent to the front lines of battle. Uriah, an elite soldier in David's army, was killed in an effort to absolve David's sin.

David then took Bathsheba to be his wife. This displeased the Lord, and Nathan was sent to rebuke David, who ultimately uttered a heartfelt cry to the Lord, "Restore to me the joy of your salvation and uphold me with a willing spirit. Then I will teach transgressors your ways and sinners will return to you . . . My tongue will sing loud of your righteousness" (Psalm 51:12–14).

The gift of God's word

We all participate in injustice actively, passively, and unintentionally. It seems we are not different from the Israelites, for we all have sinned and have fallen short of the glory of God.

What is God's response to this injustice? He shows his love for us by sending his Son to die for us while we were still sinners. He gives us a gift—Jesus.

Many different opinions, strategies, and tactics are advocated today to address the injustice that exists in our world. God has continued to place on my mind Jesus' words from the Sermon on the Mount found in Matthew 6:33. Jesus told us to focus on seeking first the kingdom of God and his righteousness.

Second Timothy 3:16–17 tells us Scripture is inspired by God and profitable for teaching, for reproof, for correction, and for training in righteousness so the man of God may be adequate, equipped for every good work.

Exhibiting justice in Christian higher education

For almost four decades, I have worked in Christian higher education at Wayland Baptist University. Obviously, I am committed to the transformative power of our mission and the work we are privileged to do.

As a Christian educator, I believe justice looks like courageously seeking out vulnerable people and helping them, educating them, and pointing them to Jesus.

Justice looks like teaching, modeling, and equipping them to understand and embrace a Christian worldview, for it is only through the redemptive work of Jesus that solutions to injustice truly are found.

We all sometimes neglect—knowingly or unknowingly— opportunities to make a difference by showing the love of Christ and pointing people to Jesus. In those times, we follow David's example—repenting and pointing back to the righteousness of God.

We cannot all do everything, but we all can do something. My part is leading, teaching, and raising the next generation to know the truth of God's love for them. Justice looks like loving God and loving others, and for me, part of loving others looks like teaching them the truth of the gospel.

Today, as injustice swirls around us, Wayland still is committed to her mission to equip her students to be a light in the darkness. Our circumstances and challenges are complex, and it often seems as if chaos reigns and that we have lost our ability to trust one another, just as humankind has done throughout history.

We often are faced with tough questions, and sometimes we may feel we don't know the answers. At Wayland during those times, with bright and expectant eyes looking back at me, I have to teach what I do know. Jesus' grace, love, and truth are the only things that truly equip us for justice.

Bobby Hall is the president of Wayland Baptist University.

64

Justice involves addressing systemic racism

Barry Creamer

I am a white man with a long history in southern, conservative Christianity. I have spoken out in recent years encouraging Americans to acknowledge ongoing racial injustice. That acknowledgment is anything but granted in white, southern society.

For those who already have a new mental model of white, Black, and American history, the remaining issue is what to do about it. Here are some ideas.

Racism as corporate, systemic problem

First, we have to address racism as a corporate, systemic problem, not just a problem of individuals gone rogue.

The question is not, How do I fix racism in America? but, In light of systemic racism's reality, what actions on my part are right?

The difference is an acknowledgment there is no utopian solution for systemic racism—a realism with two roots.

One root is that a fallen world does not admit perfect solutions. Until the eschaton, all solutions are flawed by human nature. America always will be part of a world where people tend to look askance at those who are different. Admitting America's racism does not mean it is worse than other nations.

The other root is that no solution for systemic racism will be final. We are planted in slavery's historic soil. As long as America exists, we will need group therapy in which our turn begins with, "Hi. I'm America, and I'm racist," not, "I'm American, and I'm a racist." The problem is systemic, not personal.

Hopefully, one day, instead of a confession of ongoing discrimination or oppression, it will be the humble admission that a reemergence of injustice is only one careless act away. However, admitting perfection is beyond our grasp—that systems enabling racial oppression always will be with us, even if only dormant—should not stop us from reaching for goodness.

Addressing racism individually

Second, we have to address the corporate problem as individuals. Even if I cannot make everyone else do right, I can do it myself. And the right thing for me personally will be informed by my expertise and my sphere of influence.

On expertise: While I might expand my knowledge to help more, it would be morally negligent not to use the tools already in my possession to make a difference now. We must use what we already have regardless of how unimportant it may seem because results alone do not define right and because sometimes minor acts inspire major movements.

On influence: We have the difficult task of identifying with one community while resolving tensions with another. My influence is greatest where people trust me because they identify with me.

In predominantly white, conservative churches, I have rapport and can charge headlong into controversial topics. In predominantly Black churches—though graciously welcomed—I barely tip my hat toward racial issues before stepping beyond where their trust will carry them with me. They know I do not react to police lights behind me the same way they do, so our rapport is limited.

I can and should expand my relationships, but first, I must nudge or compel people with whom I already have influence to address racial injustice where they can. Speaking for another community always either caricatures their perspective or thinly veils mine. But I can speak freely to my community now about treating others equitably.

Do what is right

Third, I myself must know and do what is right, even when others disagree. If I settle on an ethic—for instance, the golden rule—then

I can act with clarity, despite the opinions of people who may or may not agree with me or each other.

There are dangers on both sides of my ethical rail. Over one cliff—defining the right thing too conservatively—we are incapable of challenging our norms. Conserving evil with good is conservatism's intrinsic danger.

On the other side, becoming more cross-culturally aware, it also is easy to jump our ethical track—easy, but not necessary.

If I know my ethic, then I can learn from other communities, question mine, but move down the track on which God placed me. My obligation is not to conform to the disparate views of every group but, being informed by them, to do what I have found to be right.

Set an achievable goal

Finally, we need an achievable goal. Beyond our world, in the eschaton's sanctuary, inequity's deluge will cease. But here, in the community of Christ, we gather in its foyer, glimpsing into the temple itself when we worship together—a respite from the rain.

Back to daily life: though oppressive rains continue, we still can put up shelters—maybe only umbrellas—where people drenched by injustice find the brief cover of a shared meal or unsolicited support.

To do more than signal change or respond to important but impermanent movements, what we do must become part of regular life. The disadvantage: regular life is not spectacular; it grows with vegetation and melts with glaciers. The advantage: plants and glaciers shape continents.

Barry Creamer has served as president of Criswell College since 2014. He is a trained philosopher and historian with a bachelor of arts in English degree from Baylor University, a master of divinity degree from Criswell College, and a PhD in humanities from the University of Texas at Arlington.

65

Justice is reflecting God's love in public policy

Bee Moorhead

The best explanation I have heard of justice made an analogy to a machine. Justice is achieved when all the parts of the machine are interacting so each one is working optimally.

For me, this idea of justice resonates with my understanding of public policy and democracy in the way it honors both particularity and integrity.

Early in my career, I worked for the Texas Comptroller of Public Accounts writing reports. For one assignment, I had to look up the monthly employment number for a bunch of standard industrial classifications. I spent hours looking at pages and pages of tables listing occupations and suboccupations I never had heard of relating to activities I couldn't imagine.

I found myself overwhelmed by the idea there could be so many people in Texas doing so many wildly different activities. Some of them are well paid, and some are barely getting by. Some of them are doing activities that benefit the rest, while some are doing activities that probably hurt other people in some way.

Some of them are friendly, and some of them are jerks. Some are honest, some are dishonest; some are industrious, some are lazy. But they all are part of the workforce.

And I thought, "Imagine, God knows and loves every single one of those people equally."

Reflecting God's love in public policy

Justice means ordering our government, our civil society, and our personal relationships in ways that reflect God's love for each person and allow each person to thrive. One way we order our lives and relationships is through public policy.

Many people look at public policy as a kind of cage or fence put in place by an impersonal "other" either to protect us from others or to keep us from hurting them. This way of looking at policy is built on fear.

When we feel fearful, we see public policy as a way to shield ourselves from things that make us afraid. We expect law enforcement to protect us from "bad guys." We don't want people to get "more than they deserve" because that will mean less for us.

I prefer to look at public policy as a structural support that gives us the freedom to be as loving as we want to be with each other. I want to love my neighbor, but on some days, it can be hard to behave in a loving way. Public policy provides a framework of mutual responsibility that keeps us on track—that helps us "fake it till we make it."

Loving our neighbor

Public policy is about loving our neighbor. What I learned in my research project is our neighbors are many kinds of people with different needs, wants, and ideas about what's important in the world.

Looking at some of the thorniest public policy issues we face today—immigration, climate change, policing—it's apparent loving one neighbor is a lot easier than loving all of them.

It's easier to support expansive immigration policies if we ignore the real sense of displacement and disaffection some Americans feel. It's easier to support "strong border security" if we don't know any immigrants.

It's easier to support "rapid transition to renewables" if we don't know anyone who would lose their job as a result. It's easier to support pipelines if they don't cross our land.

It's easier to call for "defunding the police" if no one in our family serves in law enforcement. It's easier to support no-knock warrants if you've never been mistaken for someone else.

Justice demands we honor every member of the community as beloved of God. That doesn't mean everyone gets what they want. Public policy creates real winners and losers. But a just approach to public policy starts with the sincere belief that every person is of equal worth—even the ones we don't know or don't like.

Justice, it would seem to me, can't ignore differences. Instead, justice honors our particularities so all people can be "their best selves" without impeding any other person's opportunity to do the same.

Bee Moorhead is the executive director of Texas Impact, Texas' oldest and largest interfaith advocacy network. She also serves as an adjunct faculty member at Austin Presbyterian Theological Seminary, where she teaches faith and public policy.

66

Justice looks like the best health care for all women
Rev. Mary Whitehurst

Justice is a complicated topic for me. As an African American woman who grew up in the South, I can speak more readily to my experience with injustice.

I step outside my comfort zone here, pushing aside a painful familiarity with the ugliness of injustice, to dream optimistically about what justice could and should look like.

Justice can be defined most simply as "getting what you deserve." It is easy to think of this through the perspective of a person who commits a crime getting a "just" penalty.

Justice also looks like having your basic needs meet, getting the care you deserve, and being loved as you deserve to be loved.

In this current season of my life, justice looks like providing every underserved woman in Central Texas access to low-cost, high-quality, personalized gynecological and pregnancy health services. I am the CEO of a nonprofit women's health clinic in Austin called The Source, and this is our mission.

Our mission

I sat down last year with our leadership team to talk about why we feel called to this work. For each of us, it came down to one thing—love. God's love for us and his command for us to love others as ourselves is at the core of why we believe every woman deserves excellent health care.

The women we serve matter because they are valued and loved by the Creator of the universe, who created them in his image.

Justice looks like giving underserved women access to essential health care with providers who listen compassionately, acknowledge their concerns, and address their medical needs in a way that honors their value and worth as a person.

Racial inequality in health care

Why have I come to define justice in terms of access to health care? In our country, there are tremendous disparities in the quality of health care provided to Black and brown women, especially those below the poverty line.

What is more disheartening is, despite decades of progress, many of these inequalities are the product of our country's long, painful history of racial discrimination.

In an April 2016 University of Virginia study, researchers found "Black Americans are systematically undertreated for pain relative to white Americans."[1] The study included 418 medical students and residents.

At least half of those studied expressed some level of racial bias in their diagnosis and treatment of Black patients based on the belief that Blacks feel pain less than whites. This means there are medical professionals who falsely believe there is a biological difference in how Blacks and whites experience pain. As a result, Black patients are less likely to have their pain acknowledged, and when it is, they are prescribed less pain medication than their white counterparts.

This misinformation has been perpetuated since the time of slavery, when physicians, researchers, and slave owners justified the torture of Black slaves by subjecting them to medical experiments because of the belief Blacks had a higher threshold for pain.

A repercussion of this ignorant bias is that more Black women in Texas and throughout the United States are dying due to unaddressed complications after childbirth.

---

[1]   https://www.ncbi.nlm.nih.gov/pmc/articles/PMC4843483/ ?fbclid=IwAR0MNx2fV-SQ5N6Z63NlV6ha1z4eSCEsd5v1XANGW _1OPVhk6zD47yOnrPA.

Excellence in health care for all women

According to the Center for American Progress, "Structural racism in health care and social service delivery means that African American women often receive poorer quality care than white women. It means the denial of care when African American women seek help when enduring pain or that health care and social service providers fail to treat them with dignity and respect."[2]

I have read and heard story after story of Black women who complain of pain after childbirth having their concerns dismissed and being discharged from the hospital. They are sent home only later to suffer a stroke, heart attack, or other fatal condition. This is not what any woman deserves. This is not justice.

Justice looks like a woman walking into a women's clinic, OB-GYN's office, or hospital and being treated like a VIP-patient regardless of her color, race, ethnicity, sexual history, level of education, employment status, or ability to pay.

Justice looks like a woman's concerns being acknowledged and addressed with compassion and urgency. Justice looks like doctors, nurses, and surgeons providing all women their very best care, the care they deserve. That is what justice looks like.

Rev. Mary Whitehurst has a heart for ministering to girls and young women in crisis and currently serves as CEO of The Source, a free and low-cost women's clinic with locations in Austin and Houston.

---

[2] https://www.americanprogress.org/issues/women/reports/2019/05/02/469186/eliminating-racial-disparities-maternal-infant-mortality/.

67

Learning about injustice in home financing

Ed Francis

I did not expect to become a mortgage loan originator when I finished my master of business administration degree, and I did not take a direct path to become one. But I enjoy the work, and I am grateful.

Working in this role, I am required to do annual training about fair lending and equal credit opportunity. For many years, I have been trained to be aware of, and to avoid, discriminatory actions that result in disparate treatment or disparate impact on people of color.

Our training often has introductory comments about the legislation mandating fair lending or equal credit opportunity, but it usually omits any historical detail about the events that led up to the laws being changed.

History of unfair lending and unequal credit

These courses do not talk about property restrictions that were common for many years, stating a property could be used by "white persons only," or how the federal government intentionally imposed racial segregation through housing policy.

They don't explain that home mortgages with subsidized interest rates were readily available to veterans after World War II, unless the veteran was Black.

Nor do they teach about many desirable financing options being available to white homebuyers while they were being systematically denied too often to equally qualified Black or brown Americans.

Sadly, this is the history of home financing and home ownership in America.

I have learned these details from reading, discussions at the workplace, and, recently, from having been a part of conversations prompted by headlines about current injustices. It is not usually the story of an isolated incident of long-ago injustice, but rather the widespread and current injustices that have caught my attention.

Today, thankfully, we have much more just laws governing housing finance. How much work is left to be done to make home-ownership equitable for all people is a worthy topic for another time. My current thoughts are about these histories and the generative conversations that are possible when we, who are followers of Christ, are learning, growing, and working for change.

"Fat and sleek"

In discussions with family, friends, and business associates that have filled these days of working from home and masking up to go out, I have listened to many varying perspectives around race, opportunity, privilege, and responsibility.

Some comments have pierced my heart with doubt and sadness, but increasingly, I hear words that lift my heart with hope. I remember in my prayers all the things I have heard, and I mull them over repeatedly as I read Scripture.

In Jeremiah 5:28, the prophet tells us that the people of Judah "have grown fat and sleek. They know no limits in deeds of wickedness; they do not judge with justice the cause of the orphan, to make it prosper, and they do not defend the rights of the needy."

In the days before the pandemic, the stock market reached new highs and the economy looked unstoppable. Is that our "fat and sleek?" Maybe. I know what looked unstoppable in February 2020 when the Dow Jones hit 29,569 very quickly looked brittle and weak for a while after. So, can we really take comfort in the new higher highs?

For those willing to see, the pandemic has laid bare the fact that we too often lose sight of the orphan's cause and the rights of the needy. In our consumer-driven economy, we are being consumed by our own desires for ever-increasing levels of safety and prosperity. We want to claim our own rights but shift responsibility to others.

"Where is God leading in this?"

In these days of sickness, protest, strife, and division, when fear and doubt so easily could overwhelm, I am encouraged by the fresh conversations I hear—dialogues where differing views are expressed and greater understanding results. I sense God's movement in people seeking opportunities to hear what they have not heard and see what before they have not seen.

What is it we, who seek the kingdom of God, will do to right the injustices around us? Will we love our neighbor as ourselves by welcoming into our neighborhood those who do not look like us?

At the end of 2019, when I thought about 2020, I sure didn't foresee all that happened. When 2021 arrived, I sure hoped and prayed for better days. Through it all, I didn't expect to learn about and discuss the history of injustice in my own line of work. But I am still learning.

Where is God leading in this? I can't say for sure, but I know I have work left to do, and I am grateful for a new perspective on a job I already loved.

Ed Francis is a loan officer and sales manager in the mortgage department of a Texas-based community bank. He and his family are longtime members of Wilshire Baptist Church in Dallas.

68

Justice looks like treating all people as God's children

Jonathan Fechner

Every summer growing up, my family and I took a summer vacation. Since money wasn't growing on trees to pay for my three siblings, my parents, and me to travel by plane, we always opted for road trips.

While these road trips mostly were enjoyable, there was always at least one or two instances during the ride that caused an argument or fight between siblings, resulting in tears.

Daniel, my brother a few years older than me, was about twice my size. Doing my duty as a younger brother, I made sure to "poke the bear" the whole car ride. Eventually, he had enough, punched me in the arm as hard as he could, and I started crying to my dad for help.

My dad quickly pulled over the car, yanked Daniel out of the back seat, spanked him, and told him sternly with his finger pointed in his chest, "That is my son you just hit. Don't treat my son like that."

Having an advocate

I never will forget the feeling of having an advocate and protector. My father was fighting on my behalf, even though he knew I also had wronged my brother. My father also instilled a healthy fear in my older brother that his son was not to be abused or wronged.

What if each of us had a similar conversation with our heavenly Father? What if the Lord Almighty sternly pointed his finger in our chest demanding we treat his children with love, justice, mercy, and respect? Well, he does through Scripture.

Whether it's in Genesis at the beginning of time when he tells us mankind is created in his image or in Galatians when he proclaims believers are sons and daughters of God, these identifiers of mankind and believers point to four practical lessons that call us to seek justice, love mercy, walk humbly with our God, and to treat all people as God's children.

The sin of partiality

Partiality is a sin we often justify by saying it's just the system in which we operate. Even Christians show deference to the rich, wealthy, and powerful. We treat the esteemed with respect, give them our time and ear, and show them love and grace. But the poor we neglect, leave behind, and have no time for.

Leviticus 19:15 is clear that we are to be fair and impartial to all people, regardless of status and wealth.

- How would the world look if you treated the poor and outcasts as wealthy kings?

Rejoicing and mourning

One of the first steps to pursuing justice is to listen and empathize.

Romans 12:15 is clear when it says to "rejoice with those who rejoice; weep with those who weep." By doing so we acknowledge the individual's humanity and engage in his or her joy or sorrow.

Listening always precedes action. We must take time to listen to our brothers and sisters before we engage.

- How would the world look if you listened and empathized with all people, even those who look different than you or have totally opposite views?

Caring for the voiceless

James 1:27 shares the direct message that pure religion is caring for the orphans and widows in their distress. Orphans and widows during biblical times had no rights, no privileges, and no voice. They were unrepresented people with no one to fight on their behalf.

While we certainly are called to care for the literal orphans and widows, we also are called to practice pure religion in fighting and caring for those with no voice.

- How would the world look if you cared for those with no voice?

Sharing all things in common

The last call for justice is for communities of Christian believers. Acts 2 commands believers to share possessions, food, fellowship, and worship with one another, to have all things in common.

If believers did this, it would be a compelling example of the benefits of a Christian lifestyle and the greatest evangelistic tool one could use. We would create an equitable lifestyle among our brothers and sisters in Christ, thereby encouraging others to participate.

- How would the world look if you shared all things in common with your brothers and sisters in Christ?

Through being impartial, rejoicing and mourning, caring for the voiceless, and sharing all things in common, we truly can seek justice, love mercy, and honor every human as image-bearers of God.

Jonathan Fechner is the Chief of Staff at Dallas Baptist University, executive director of DBU's Institute for Global Engagement, and president of BridgeBuilders, a nonprofit working in South Dallas to provide student services, job training, and community empowerment. Jonathan is a proud alumnus of Dallas Baptist University.

69

Justice goes hand in hand with righteousness

Justin Lawrence

The greatest problems with Christianity today are people who acknowledge Jesus with their lips and deny him by their lifestyle and people who have reduced God to a political party.

God is not a Republican or a Democrat. He is the King of the universe. All true authority belongs to him, and he is not handing out wholesale endorsements to either party because there are unbiblical positions both parties promote. He is equally concerned about those issues.

Injustice exists in American Christianity for two main reasons. First, the love of a political party trumps God's command to love our neighbor. Second, society has taken a side for righteousness or justice, with one outweighing the other.

Righteousness underlies justice

Righteousness is the underlying principle of justice. Without righteousness, there can be no justice.

Justice is the application of righteousness. In God's kingdom, righteousness and justice always must be found side by side without tilting either way.

Psalm 89:14 says righteousness and justice come from God's throne. You never choose righteousness or justice. They always must walk side by side.

Choosing one over the other has led to the great divide among believers. Look no further than the following:

- Christians using divisive language on social media platforms, telling us we can't be Christian if we don't vote for a certain party.
- Christians believing God prioritizes and only is concerned about the life of unborn babies, but not babies, children, teens, and adults outside of the womb.
- Christians claiming to be pro-life while putting the economy over humanity or not being willing to wear a mask, social distance, or otherwise sacrifice during the pandemic to save a life.
- Christians trying to legislate morality through the courts and city ordinances instead of obeying Jesus' instruction in the Great Commission to teach his commands (Matthew 28:16–20) or to love as he commanded in the Great Commandment (Matthew 22:36–40).

God wants us to be right with him, and he also wants us to be right with each other. Whenever we choose between the two, we miss the heart of God.

Justice is individual and communal

Justice, as defined with righteousness, is not restricted to the role of legal institutions. Justice is concerned with restoring harmony to the community. It involves acting for community members and against oppressors. It tries to improve situations rather than simply giving out what people deserve. It struggles to create wholeness where currently there are pressing needs.

An illustration of such justice appears in Job 29:7–25. Job describes how he "put on righteousness, and it clothed me; my justice was like a robe and a turban" (29:14). He did this by rescuing the poor and the fatherless; comforting the dying; supporting widows; helping the blind, lame, and needy; serving as an advocate of the stranger; and opposing those who would take advantage of others (29:12–13, 15–17).

Biblical justice actively pursues the welfare of the community and the individuals in it. It is the responsibility of Christians and the church, not merely the judiciary.

Justice consists of concrete actions of caring. It moves beyond written laws and ordinances to address weakness, poverty, and inequities of every kind. This is what justice has in common with righteousness.

Righteousness can be described as virtue in action, or the intent to do what is right. It refers to the quality of relationships between individuals. Justice in its parallel meaning addresses both the victim and the situation that created the need; righteousness draws attention to the character of the helper.

Justice and righteousness are inseparable

"Keep justice, and do righteousness, for my salvation is about to come, and my righteousness to be revealed. Blessed is the man who does this, and the son of man who lays hold on it; who keeps from defiling the Sabbath, and keeps his hand from doing any evil" (Isaiah 56:1–2).

Isaiah's message is consistent in theme and tone. He preaches social justice and personal righteousness as the proof of salvation. The very fact Isaiah reversed the terms from an earlier prophecy and put justice ahead of righteousness reinforces the inseparability of the two.

Whether justice or righteousness comes first in Isaiah's listing is incidental to the fact they are inseparable. You cannot have one without the other or promote one at the expense of the other.

Justin Lawrence, Esq., is professor of justice administration and legal studies, Title IX administrator, and associate dean of the School of Behavioral and Social Science at Wayland Baptist University.

INDEX OF SUBJECTS

16th Avenue Baptist Church, Birmingham, Ala., 40

Abilene Christian University, 120
abolition, 69, 159
abortion, pro-life, 216
abundance, 171-73, 183
abuse, 31, 32, 34, 59, 110, 135, 149, 158, 165, 189-90, 212
accountability, 101, 102, 105, 143, 144, 163
action, doing, 3, 17-19, 34, 55, 57, 63, 65-66, 68, 69, 75, 80, 84, 85, 87, 89, 91, 98, 102, 104, 105, 107-8, 115, 122, 123, 126, 131, 139, 144, 146, 152, 154, 163, 175, 177, 178, 179, 190, 200, 209, 213, 217
activist, 40, 115, 132, 133, 164
Acts 17 Apologetics, 84
addiction, alcoholism, 167-69, 191
Addis Ababa, Ethiopia, 127
Admission Review and Dismissal, 14-15
adolescent: see youth
adoption, 14-15
advocate, advocacy, 13, 14-16, 29, 65, 75, 109, 111, 116, 144, 163; see also plead
Africa, African, 9, 28, 40, 63, 95, 136-38
African American: see Black
African American Fellowship, 29
African American Ministries, 123

Agape Baptist Church, Fort Worth, Tex., 100
age, ageism, 35, 105
Aguirre, Rolando, 174-76
alcohol, alcoholism: see addiction
all lives matter, 87, 122, 137-38
America, American, 3, 10, 12, 13, 20, 25, 28, 29, 30, 31, 32, 34, 40, 52, 65, 71-73, 80, 86, 93, 94, 96, 97, 98, 127-29, 131, 132, 136, 142, 143, 157, 160, 162n4, 181, 182, 183, 189, 200, 204, 208, 210, 215; see also United States
American Dream, 86
American history, 12-13, 128, 200
Amos (biblical person), 195
anger, 3, 17-19, 106, 148, 151-52, 183
anti-racism, 80-82, 93
apartheid, 136-38
Arab, Arabic, 23-26
Arbery, Ahmaud, 1, 41, 115, 123, 189
arrest, 41, 42, 71, 165, 168
Asian, Asian American, 28, 95, 157
Asian American Christian Collaborative, 52
assimilation, 72
assault, 40, 41, 145, 165, 190
asylum, 30-32, 44-45, 181
Atlantic, the, 65
attorney, lawyer, 9, 37, 41, 42, 63, 64, 104, 105, 118, 165, 169, 194
Aulds, Cynthia, 101-3
Austin, Tex., 22, 63, 163, 183, 206, 208

219

Austin Presbyterian Theological Seminary, 205
authority, authorities, 1, 25, 27, 39, 77, 91, 149, 154, 159, 215
awakening, 145–47, 152
Aylward, Gladys, 69

baby, babies, infant, infants, 69, 125, 182–83, 208n2, 216; *see also* child, children
Baby Suggs, 130–31
Bailey Robinson, Rev. Cokiesha, 93–95
bank, 143, 172, 211
Baptist General Convention of Texas (BGCT), 3, 29, 49, 73, 123, 141, 156; *see also* Texas Baptists
Baptist Standard, 1, 2, 4, 32, 150
Baptist Student Ministry, 149
Baptist Studies Center, Abilene Christian University, 120
Baptist Temple, San Antonio, 66
Baptist University of the Américas, 54–57
Baptists, 1, 8, 10, 26, 126
Barna, 153
Bartimaeus (biblical person), 63
Bathsheba, 197
Baylor University, 10, 42, 70, 82, 92, 98, 126, 147, 160, 173, 202
Be the Bridge, 190
Bedilu, Levi, 127–29
Bell, Rev. Debra, 142–44
Bell, Derrick, 115
Bell, Michael, 164–66
belonging, 7, 10, 24, 94, 106, 190
Beloved, 130–31, 132
Bender, Kimlyn, 67–70
Bethlehem Baptist Church, Mansfield, 73
betrayal, 28, 152
bias, biased, biases, 41, 42, 62, 66, 145, 147, 151, 166, 207
Bible study, 152, 167
biblical justice, 25, 61–62, 168, 175, 217
bigotry, 72, 135
Black, African American, 1, 15, 18, 20, 28, 29, 40–42, 65, 71, 72, 73, 74, 78, 80–81, 86–87, 90, 95, 97, 100, 102, 109, 111, 113, 115n2, 121, 122, 123, 125–26, 127–29, 130–32, 133,

137–38, 142–44, 154–55, 157–59, 164–65, 166, 167, 181–83, 188, 189, 190, 200–201, 206–8, 209
Black, Eric, 1–4, 53, 55
Black church, 29, 128–29, 201
Black Codes, 28
Black History Month, 87
Black Lives Matter, Black lives matter, 28, 40–42, 72, 87, 121, 123, 137, 144
Black's Law Dictionary, 105
A Black Theology of Liberation, 158
The Bluest Eye, 130, 132
bond, bail, 165, 168, 182
Bonhoeffer, Dietrich, 122
Booker-Drew, Froswa', 17–19
border, U.S./Mexico, 30–32, 43–46, 59, 77–78, 150, 157, 169, 204
Border Patrol, immigration enforcement, 44
Botswana, 136
boycott, 164
Brambila, Ricardo, 77–79
Brazil, 58
Bread Fellowship, 13
bribe, 83, 195
BridgeBuilders, 214
Brock, Pastor Kan'Dace, 86-88
brother, 18, 25, 44–46, 52, 58, 66, 73, 80, 87, 88, 90, 93, 96, 117, 124, 125, 134, 135, 139, 154, 169, 184–87, 212, 213, 214; *see also* sibling; family
Brother Bill's Helping Hand, 134–35
brown, 71, 72, 86, 87, 142, 143, 167, 207, 209
Brueggemann, Walter, 11, 171
Buckner Family Hope Center, 60, 79
Buckner International, 19, 39, 59, 137, 138

California, 32, 108, 140
calling, 3, 4, 7, 13, 18, 21, 22, 26, 38, 41, 44, 47, 68, 69, 81–82, 92, 100, 107, 110, 111, 115, 122, 126, 141, 153n3, 156, 158, 160, 168, 169, 175, 179, 183, 191, 193, 195, 206, 213, 214
cancel culture, 64
Cano, Anyra, 109–12
Cape Town, South Africa, 136
capital murder, 104, 177, 179

Index of Subjects — 221

capital punishment, 162

Catholic, 23, 109, 157

Center for Church and Community
Impact, 92

Central Texas, 106, 206

Chang, Raymond, 52

change, 21, 29, 30, 31, 32, 35, 52, 60n3,
69, 94, 98, 102, 129, 131, 133, 143n4,
144, 146, 152, 163, 179, 182, 192,
193, 202, 204, 209, 210

Chauvin, Derek, 1, 41

checking account, 59

child, children, 10, 11–13, 14–16, 24,
27, 30, 31–32, 34, 41, 45, 46, 58, 59,
60, 61, 72, 74, 77–78, 79, 80, 81, 86,
89–90, 91, 102, 106–8, 113–14, 123,
125, 126, 134, 139, 141, 145, 161,
169, 174, 181, 191, 192, 212–14, 216;
see also baby, babies, infant, infants

child of God, children of God, 41, 80,
81, 91, 212–14

childbirth, 126, 207–8

China, 69

Chrisman, Os, 117–18

Christ, 3, 4, 9, 18, 19, 21, 22, 23, 25, 29,
37, 38, 43–46, 52, 62, 66, 67, 68–69,
81, 93, 96, 105, 107, 110–11, 114,
122, 126, 128, 129, 131, 133, 134,
135, 142–43, 150, 151–52, 168, 174–
75, 179, 180, 183, 185, 186, 187, 196,
198, 202, 210, 214; *see also* Jesus

Christian, Christianity, 3, 4, 7, 8, 9, 10,
22, 23–26, 38, 41, 46, 51–52, 53, 54,
55, 57, 60, 66, 67–70, 73, 76, 89, 90,
103, 107, 108, 109, 112, 113, 115,
117, 118, 120, 128, 133, 134, 135,
141, 145–46, 147, 151, 156, 158, 169,
170, 171n1, 178–79, 181, 183, 184,
185, 190, 198, 200, 213, 214, 215–17

Christian Community Development
Association (CCDA), 43

Christian Latina Leadership Institute
(CLLI), 54, 55, 57, 112

Christian Life Commission (Texas
Baptists), 76, 141, 183

Christian nationalism, 181

church, churches, ekklesia, 3, 16, 17,
18, 19, 22, 23, 25, 26, 28–29, 37, 39,
40, 44–45, 52, 54, 63, 67, 68, 69, 70,
73, 80, 85, 88, 89, 90, 91, 92, 94, 96,
97, 98, 100, 101, 103, 105, 106–8,
110, 111, 122, 123, 124, 125, 128–29,
133, 134, 135, 140, 142–44, 148, 150,
151–52, 153, 157–60, 166, 167–70,
173, 176, 184–87, 190, 193, 196, 201,
211, 217

Church Under the Bridge, Waco, 133,
167–70

Church Without Walls, the, Houston,
144

citation, ticket, 164

citizen, citizenship, 12, 21, 23, 24, 52,
69, 71, 109, 142, 145, 155, 181

Ciudad Nueva Community Outreach,
46

civil rights, Civil Rights Act, civil rights
movement, 28, 40, 64, 69, 132, 133,
143, 159, 164

Civilian Conservation Corps, 124

class, 12, 24, 72, 125, 167, 196

climate change, 30, 32, 182, 204

clothes, clothing, 44, 48, 61, 216

Coalition to Combat Human
Trafficking in Texas, 103

coercion, 101, 102

Cole, Carl, 162

Collaborative on Hunger and Poverty,
98

Collins, Scott, 136–38

colonias, 77

Colossae, 184–86

command, commandment, 11, 18, 21,
45, 64, 115–16, 123, 133, 194, 206,
214, 215–16

community, communities, 8, 10, 12, 13,
19, 22, 34, 35, 39, 40, 41, 46, 50, 54,
60, 71, 77, 81, 83, 86, 91, 92, 94, 96,
98, 102, 107, 109, 110, 111, 113, 115,
116, 117, 118, 120, 133, 135, 145,
146, 152, 157–60, 161, 163, 164, 165,
166, 168, 169, 170, 173, 176, 178,
179, 182, 184, 190, 192, 201, 202,
205, 211, 214, 216–17

compassion, 48–49, 63, 67, 69, 74–76,
110, 122, 153, 162, 175, 178, 207,
208

Cone, James, 9, 158–59

confess, confession, 51, 145, 148, 149,
190, 201

conscientization, 146

222 — Index of Subjects

conservative, 96, 200, 201, 202
constitution, state, 13
Constitution, U.S., 64, 142, 157
control, 37, 39, 62, 63, 189
convict: *see* prison, prisoner
conviction, 12, 40, 42, 59, 67, 74, 76, 104, 105, 134, 152, 156, 182, 190
Cooper, Amy, 65–66
Cooperative Baptist Fellowship, 32, 36, 42, 76, 183
Cornerstone Baptist Church, Dallas, 19
Corona, Ali, 188–90
corrupt, corruption, 62, 77, 84, 151
Cotton, Roy, 121–23
Council on Alcohol and Drug Abuse of the Coastal Bend, 85
counseling, counselor, 169, 190, 191, 193; *see also* therapy, therapist
court, 44, 50 51, 117–18, 151, 163, 165, 177, 216
court-appointed special advocate, 75
covenant, 6, 171, 176
COVID-19, 3, 59, 86, 97, 104, 153, 162, 172, 181n3; *see also* pandemic
Creamer, Barry, 200–202
creation, created, 1–2, 5, 7, 11, 12, 18, 37, 53, 55, 59, 62, 67–68, 73, 117, 121, 123, 134, 175, 182, 183, 185, 207, 212
crime, 9, 30, 40, 42, 105, 155, 161, 166, 177–79, 182, 206
criminal justice, 28, 165, 166, 178, 179
Criswell College, Dallas, 202
cross, crucifixion, 9–10, 43, 67, 68, 78, 100, 174–76, 185
The Cross and the Lynching Tree, 9–10, 100
culture, cultural, 20, 21, 26, 32, 38, 39, 49, 50, 52, 64, 67, 69, 81, 87, 93, 94, 107, 108, 125, 127, 128, 150 152, 153, 160, 165, 167, 168, 173, 174, 175, 176, 187, 189, 202
Cypress-Fairbanks Independent School District, 29

Dale, Randy, 104–5
Dallas, 1, 19, 79, 118, 134, 135, 147, 176, 211, 214
Dallas Baptist University, 116, 126, 141, 160
David (king of Israel), 68, 197–98

David Chapel Missionary Baptist Church, Austin, 63
De La Torre, Miguel, 146
death, 71, 111, 117, 119, 161, 162, 174, 183, 188, 189
death row, 161–63
Declaration of Independence, 117, 123, 142, 157
deed restrictions, 64
Deer, Sarah, 51
defend, defense, 6, 104, 120, 131, 134, 145, 179, 180, 210
defendant, 177–79
defund the police, 83, 205
deliverance, 22, 117, 119, 180
democracy, 32, 158, 182, 203
demonstration, demonstrator, 28, 71, 165
Department of Homeland Security, 31
desegregation, 65, 135
DeYmaz, Mark, 153
Diana R. Garland School of Social Work (Baylor), 82, 92
DiAngelo, Robin, 137
dignity, 21, 37, 39, 47, 49, 67, 68, 69, 75, 81, 89, 90, 95, 110, 131, 144, 182, 208
din, 6
disability, disabled, 95, 192
disadvantage, 143, 159–60, 202
disciple, disciples, discipleship, followers of Christ, 2, 3, 4, 10, 21, 22, 25, 38, 39, 48, 49, 53, 62, 65, 67, 89, 105, 110, 111, 119, 120, 122, 134, 144, 155–56, 168, 174, 175, 183, 187, 193, 210
discrimination, 19, 22, 28, 37, 62, 107, 125, 165, 201, 207, 209
disfranchisement, disenfranchisement, 165, 182
diversity, equity, inclusion (DEI), 10, 29, 39, 71–73, 87, 93–95
doctors, 207–8
domestic violence, 190
Donne, John, 172
Dorrell, Jimmy, 167–70
Douglass, Frederick, 131
Down syndrome, 14
Doyle, Pastor Samuel, 184–87
driving while Black (DWB), 137
Du Bois, W.E.B., 131, 132

Index of Subjects — 223

due process, 117–18
drugs, 85, 91, 155, 169, 191

Earth, 2, 11, 12, 19, 21, 38, 53, 54, 69,
  116, 120, 151–53, 183
East Texas Baptist University, College,
  7, 124, 126
economics, economy, 2, 13, 21, 29,
  33, 34, 35, 51, 91, 93, 105, 117, 128,
  143n5, 159, 165, 173, 181n2, 210 216
education, 2, 11–13, 14, 15–16, 28, 35,
  36, 41, 52, 54, 59, 72, 76, 91, 98, 101,
  111, 124, 125, 134, 144, 156, 161,
  182n6, 198, 208
EduK Child Strategies, 60
El Paso, Tex., 43–46
emancipation, 185
empathy, 48, 110, 145–46, 183
The Emperor's New Clothes, 61
employment, 42, 84, 91, 97, 140, 169,
  203, 208; *see also* job; labor; work
empower, empowerment, 111, 114,
  131, 169, 214
end times, eschatology, 25, 200, 202
English, 23, 132, 140, 146, 149, 202
environment, 14, 65, 77, 78, 79, 204
Ephesus, 37, 184–87
equal, equality, 7, 12, 23, 24, 29, 31,
  33, 35, 73, 81, 83, 94, 100, 107, 117,
  121, 123, 132, 133, 141, 151, 164,
  165, 181, 182, 183, 185, 203, 205,
  209, 215
Equal Justice Initiative, 113
Equiano, Olaudah, 69
equitable, equity, 6, 12, 13, 23, 27, 29,
  55, 59, 62, 76, 93, 94, 106, 107, 108,
  111, 115, 132, 142, 143, 144, 151,
  156, 164–66, 171, 182n7, 183n14,
  194, 201, 210 214
Erickson, Millard, 53, 55
ethics, ethical, 5, 6, 21, 37, 64, 70, 120,
  131, 156, 158n2, 185, 191, 201–2; *see
  also* moral, morality
Ethiopia, Ethiopian, Ethiopian
  American, 65, 127–28, 129
ethnic, ethnicity, 2, 15, 39, 62, 63, 72,
  77, 78, 107, 108, 109, 129, 140, 153,
  165, 166, 182n8, 183n14, 208
evangelical, evangelicalism, 23, 25,
  115n2, 129, 153, 160, 189
Evangelical Immigration Table, 153

Evans, Rev. Dr. Michael, Sr., 71–73
Evans, Tony, 143
Everett, Jeremy, 96–98
evil, evildoers, 29, 66, 121, 122, 128,
  132, 158, 175, 180, 195, 202, 217
execution, 161–63
Exodus, book, 7, 171, 173
exploitation, 62, 80, 91
extortion, 30, 32

fair, fairly, fairness, 23, 31, 32, 33, 34,
  47, 48, 53, 62, 80, 81, 90, 102, 105,
  106, 107, 115, 122, 125, 130, 131,
  139, 140, 141, 142, 144, 151, 154,
  155, 158, 163, 168, 174, 181, 194,
  209, 213
faith, religious, 1, 3, 4, 8, 32, 35, 45, 47,
  59, 60, 69, 80, 86, 97, 98, 105, 109,
  120, 128, 131–32, 133, 140, 142–43,
  146, 157, 176, 178, 185, 205
family, families, 11, 15, 22, 24, 30–32,
  33–34, 39, 42, 54, 57, 58–60, 69, 80,
  90, 93, 98, 106, 109, 110, 114, 115,
  117–18, 124–26, 132, 139, 140, 161–
  63, 165, 174, 176, 177–79, 181, 182,
  186, 187, 191, 200, 210, 211, 212
father, Father (God), 4, 24, 27, 32, 73,
  85, 87, 89–90, 114, 149, 161, 162n3,
  187, 212; *see also* parent, parents
fatherless, 24, 122, 134, 175, 216
favor, 1, 3, 134, 151, 152
fear, 34, 45, 63, 72, 87, 125, 135, 137,
  155, 158, 166, 173, 183, 192, 196,
  204, 211, 212
Fechner, Jonathan, 212–14
Federalist Papers, 158
Fellowship Southwest, 31, 32, 112, 183
felon, felony, 117, 155, 165, 182
finances, 59, 65, 129, 169, 210; *see also*
  income; money
First Amendment, 164
First Baptist Church, Marble Falls, 190
First Baptist Church, Temple, 105
First Baptist Church, Weslaco, 108
First Metropolitan Church, Houston,
  29
First Woodway Baptist Church, Waco,
  92
Florida, 41
Floyd, George, 1, 22, 28, 41, 71, 115,
  123, 143, 189

224 — Index of Subjects

food, groceries, 31, 48, 59, 63, 96, 97, 134, 167, 169, 180, 181, 214
food desert, 63, 169
forgive, forgiveness, 7, 35, 85, 94, 152
formerly incarcerated, 134
foster, fostering, 15
Foster, Ferrell, 154–56
Francis, Ed, 209–11
fraud, 101, 102
freedom, 28, 30, 31, 38, 58–60, 75, 81, 111, 114, 126, 130, 131, 134, 138, 142, 158, 182, 201, 204
friends, friendship, 15, 18, 24, 34, 35, 64, 65, 66, 72, 90, 93, 106, 115, 123, 124–25, 126, 132, 137, 140, 150, 162, 167, 169, 192, 203, 210

gang, gangs, 30–32, 33, 40, 44, 161
Garner, Eric, 123
gaslighting, 189
Gaston Christian Center, Dallas, 147
gender, 2, 12, 15, 34, 35, 62, 63, 105, 117
Generous Justice, 27–28
Geronimus, Arline, 125
gerrymandering, 28, 182
GLOO, 153
God, 1, 3, 4, 5, 6, 7, 9, 10, 11–12, 17, 18–19, 20–22, 24, 25, 27–28, 37–39, 41, 45, 48, 49, 50, 52, 53–57, 60, 62, 64, 65, 67–69, 73, 74, 75, 76, 77, 78, 79, 80, 81–82, 88, 89, 91–92, 94, 100, 102–3, 104–5, 106, 107, 108, 109–10, 115, 116, 119–20, 121–22, 125, 126, 128, 134, 135, 140, 141, 143–44, 151–53, 156, 157, 158–59, 160, 167, 168, 172, 173, 174–76, 182, 183, 184, 185, 187, 190n2, 191, 193, 194, 195, 196, 197–98, 202, 203–5, 206, 211, 212–14, 215, 216
God's will, 18–19, 21, 53–54, 151–53
Golden Rule, 123, 196, 201–2
good, 8–9, 13, 24, 27, 29, 49, 62, 65, 69–70, 75, 81, 84–85, 94, 100, 101–3, 105, 110–11, 118, 126, 131, 134, 140, 146–47, 155, 162, 166, 171, 175, 176, 178, 180, 185, 186, 191, 195–96, 198, 201, 202
Good Samaritan, 8–10, 65, 146–47

Goodyear, Jack, 157–60
gospel, good news, 8, 17, 25, 49, 62, 81, 90, 91, 94, 107, 110, 131, 134, 159, 185, 186, 187, 196, 198
govern, government, 5, 30, 33, 45, 96, 124, 204, 209, 210
grace, 35, 54, 67, 84, 85, 105, 125, 140, 178, 185, 199, 213
Grace College & Seminary, Winona, Ill., 95
Graham, Billy, 176
grammar, 149
grandparent, grandparents, 123, 127, 149; *see also* family
Great Commandment, 8, 64, 116, 194, 216
Great Commission, 216
Greater New Light Missionary Baptist Church, Waco, 187
Greater St. Stephen First Baptist Church, Fort Worth, 166
The Greatest Story Ever Told, 9
greed, 32, 47, 101, 151
Green, Nell, 33–36
greenlining, 64–65
grief, mourning, 3, 81, 94, 151, 188–90, 213, 214
Guillen, Vanessa, 22
guilt, 51, 81, 105, 122, 177, 179
Gushee, David & Glen Stassen, 21

Habitat for Humanity, 75
Haiti, 135, 169
Hall, Bobby, 197–99
Harper, Lisa Sharon, 110
harass, harassment, 63, 72, 164
hate, 17, 18, 29, 62, 64, 84, 135, 195
heal, healing, 22, 34, 35, 38, 51, 62, 65, 74, 75, 96–98, 110, 137, 163, 175, 189, 191, 192
health, 2, 35, 59, 71, 75, 76, 83–85, 93, 97, 110, 111, 125, 134, 156, 169, 183n12, 183n14, 191, 206
health care, 28, 35, 63, 96, 126, 169, 173, 182, 183n14, 206–8
Hearne, Latisha Waters, 113–16
heaven, 18, 19, 21, 38, 69, 129, 151–53, 183, 187, 190, 212
Henry, Michelle, 130–32

Index of Subjects — 225

Hereford, Tex., 148–49
Hetey, Rebecca and Jennifer L.
   Eberhardt, 165–66
Higgins, Jessie, 191–93
Hispanic, 15, 22, 77, 87, 97, 102, 106,
   126, 141, 149–50, 157
Hispanic Baptist Convention of Texas,
   Convención Bautista Hispana de
   Texas, 22, 150
Hitler, Adolf, 171
Holy Spirit, 4, 38, 44, 53–54, 56, 134,
   135, 152, 156, 168
Home, 131, 132
homeless, 117, 167, 169
homeowner, 209–10
honest, honesty, 37, 131, 203
honor, 55, 57, 89, 90, 130, 156, 176,
   203, 205, 207, 214
hope, hopeless, hopelessness, 3, 4, 10,
   12, 24, 33–36, 38, 54, 60, 63, 68–70,
   72, 78, 79, 89, 96, 109, 111, 118, 128–
   29, 131, 156, 157, 185, 201, 210, 211
*Hope Now: Peace, Healing, and Justice
   When the Kingdom Comes Near*, 38
hospital, 24, 208
hospitality, 8, 9, 10, 181
Houle Cuellar, Kristin, 161–63
housing, housing discrimination, 28,
   33, 48, 64–65, 75, 77, 91, 169, 181,
   195, 209–10
Houston Christian University
   (formerly Houston Baptist
   University), 144, 196
Hughes, Langston, 157, 160
human, humanity, humanness, 5, 6,
   11–12, 20–21, 25, 27, 28, 36, 44, 45,
   53, 55, 62, 64, 67–69, 73, 75, 78, 80,
   86, 88, 91, 94, 101, 102, 103, 105,
   110, 115, 117, 119, 123, 128, 131,
   132, 134, 135, 137, 158, 159, 163,
   172, 175, 194, 196, 198, 200, 213,
   214, 216, 217
human rights, 12, 45, 132
human trafficking, 36, 101–3
humble, humility, 4, 27, 41, 51, 62, 67,
   81, 94, 115, 126, 153, 160, 175, 190,
   196, 197, 201, 213
humiliation, 149, 150
Humphreys, Jean, 124–26

Humphries, Mariah, 50–52
hunger, hungry, 43, 48, 96, 97, 98, 134,
   180, 181

idealism, 100
Iglesia Bautista Victoria en Cristo, Fort
   Worth, 112
image of God, 5, 37, 41, 67–68, 73, 77,
   89, 110, 121, 128, 172
immigrant, immigration, 8, 22, 30–32,
   78, 109, 111, 117, 148–49, 153, 157,
   204; *see also* migrant
impartiality, 61, 105, 118, 142, 144,
   213, 214
implicit bias, 41–42
incarceration, 8, 28, 45, 62, 113, 134,
   162, 165–66, 169, 182
inclusion, 29, 87, 91, 93–95
income, 93, 96–97, 102, 125–26, 140,
   169, 192; *see also* finances; money
incremental, 100
India, 169
Indian Removal Act, 50
Indigenous: *see* Native, Native
   American
inequality, inequity, unequal, 39, 66,
   107, 113, 143n5, 181n2, 181n4, 196,
   202, 207
institution, institutions, 3, 13, 37, 39,
   62, 166, 184, 187, 216
insurance, 169, 193
interest, 172, 181, 209
Introducing Christian Doctrine, 53, 55
investigation, 41, 151, 179
invite, invitation, 1, 3, 9, 10, 43, 48, 53–
   57, 106, 150, 167, 169
Ireland, David D., 152, 153
Isaiah (biblical person), 156, 179, 195,
   217
isolation, 120, 172, 191, 210
Israel, Israeli, 7, 23–26, 29, 79, 119,
   171, 195, 197

Jackson, Andrew (U.S. President), 50
Jacobs, Harriet, 131
jail, 155, 165, 182
Jeroboam II (king of Israel), 195
Jesus, 2, 3, 4, 8–10, 14, 17, 18, 21, 23–
   24, 25–26, 29, 32, 34, 35, 38, 39, 43,
   45, 47–49, 51, 62–63, 64, 65, 66, 73,

74, 75, 78–79, 89, 91, 100, 110–11, 114, 119, 120, 122, 123, 126, 134, 135, 137, 138, 140–41, 146, 155–56, 159, 174–75, 186, 187, 190, 193, 196, 197–99, 215, 216; *see also* Christ

Jesus and the Disinherited, 159

Jews, Jewish, 9, 23–25, 65, 69, 109, 111, 114, 126, 134, 146–47

Jim Crow, 28, 142–43

Job (biblical person), 216

job, 15, 24, 31, 32, 59, 65, 71, 93, 97, 126, 134, 169, 191, 204, 211, 214; *see also* employment; labor; work

job training, 134, 169, 214

Johnson, Charles Foster, 11–13

Johnson, James Weldon, 72–73

Jordan, Barbara, 117

Joseph (biblical person), 171–72

joy, 15, 18, 30, 54, 75, 139, 151, 180, 197, 209, 213

Jubilee Food Market, 169

jubilee year, 7

judge, judgment, 5–6, 16, 37, 42, 48, 67, 68, 79, 104, 117–18, 119–20, 174, 196, 210

jury, 41, 162

Just Mercy: A Story of Justice and Redemption, 33

justice system, 28, 41, 145, 152, 165, 166, 178

justification, justified, 41, 45, 67–70, 146, 151, 172, 195, 207, 213

juvenile justice, 163

Keller, Tim, 27–28

Keyes, Wes, 133–35

killing, 1, 15, 30, 31, 33, 40, 72, 143, 161–63, 177, 178, 197; *see also* murder

kindness, 32, 51, 67, 94, 126, 162, 175, 176

King, Dr. Martin Luther, Jr., 42, 59–60, 65, 95, 99, 100, 132, 144, 158, 176

kingdom, of God, 19, 20–22, 29, 37–39, 60, 65, 69, 82, 110, 119, 175–76, 183, 186, 190, 198, 211, 215

Kingdom Ethics, 21

Kirk, Brenda, 151–53

Knowing Christ Today: Why We Can Trust Spiritual Knowledge, 150

Knox, Marv, 30–32

Ku Klux Klan, KKK, 28, 40

labor, 30, 34, 69, 101, 102; *see also* employment; job; work

labor trafficking, 102

Lady Justice (statue), 61, 151

lament, 81, 94, 190

Lane, Patty, 47–49

Latina, Latino, Latinx, 20, 22, 28, 54, 55, 56–57, 95, 97, 109, 112, 150, 181, 182–83

law (God's), 3, 21, 47, 53, 64, 78, 104–5, 111, 146, 174, 194, 196

law (human), legislation, legislative, 13, 21, 24, 37, 41, 42, 64, 83, 102, 109, 111, 117–18, 137, 142–43, 150, 151, 155, 162, 165, 166, 183, 193, 209, 210, 216, 217

law and order, 83

law enforcement, 2, 37, 40, 83–85, 87, 139, 151, 155, 164, 165, 177, 179, 204, 205; *see also* police

Lawrence, Justin, 215–17

lawsuit, litigation, 109, 165

lawyer: *see* attorney

least of these, 8, 32, 43, 45, 46, 73, 122, 180, 192

legislator, legislators, 163, 209

leper, 65, 175

Lewis, C.S., 122

Lewis, John (Congressman), 123, 132, 196

LGBTQ+, 102

liberation, 81, 131

liberation theology, 131, 145–46, 158–59

liberty, 12, 28, 29, 62, 117, 142, 183

lie, lying, 31, 173, 189

"Lift Every Voice and Sing," 72–73

listen, 2, 3, 20, 21, 29, 55, 81, 111, 127, 133, 161, 167, 189, 190, 207, 210, 213

The Little Book of Biblical Justice, 61–62

Livingston, Tex., 162

loan, lending, 28, 63, 64, 75, 143, 169, 172, 181, 209–11

Locke, Alain, 131

Long Walk to Freedom, 138

Lord's Prayer, 19, 38

Index of Subjects — 227

love, 4, 9, 11, 12, 14, 15, 18–19, 21, 22, 27, 29, 30, 31, 32, 37, 41, 44–45, 48, 51, 62, 64, 65, 66, 69, 73, 77, 80, 81, 85, 89, 90, 91, 94, 103, 107, 115, 116, 117, 119, 126, 129, 130–31, 132, 135, 142, 144, 145, 150, 151, 153, 156, 160, 174, 175, 177, 178–79, 184–87, 193, 194, 195–96, 197, 198, 199, 203–5, 206–7, 211, 212–13, 214, 215, 216
Lozano, Nora, 53–57
lynching, 9–10, 28, 40, 100, 132, 143

Madison, James, 158
man, men, male, 1, 5, 6, 10, 12, 15, 27, 34, 35, 40, 41, 42, 48, 65, 71, 72, 94, 95, 100, 105, 110, 111, 117, 119, 120, 123, 125, 126, 131, 133, 134, 135, 136, 137–38, 145, 146–47, 152, 155, 157, 161–63, 167, 172, 175, 176, 184–87, 192, 195, 196, 198, 200, 217
Mandela, Nelson, 136, 138
manipulation, 189
Mansfield, Tex., 73
Maranatha International Church, Houston, 196
marginalized, 22, 24, 77, 80, 91, 110, 111, 121, 165, 168, 178
marriage, 11, 90–91, 124–25
Marshall, Chris, 61–62
Martin, Trayvon, 41, 143
martyr, 122, 185
Maslow, Abraham, 12
mass incarceration, 8, 28, 113, 182
media, news, 2, 41, 51, 64, 65, 72, 96, 104, 121, 135, 172, 177, 216
medication, 192, 207
mental health, 59, 134, 167, 168, 169, 190, 191–93
mentor, mentoring, 104, 116, 162
mercy, 21, 22, 24, 27, 35, 41, 62, 67, 105, 115, 118, 133, 140, 146, 153, 160, 178, 185, 190, 196, 212, 213, 214
A Mercy, 131, 132
meshar, 6–7
The Message Church, San Antonio, 88
Mexican, 31, 148–50
Mexico, 31, 32, 43, 44, 59, 149
Mexico City, 169

Meyer Center for Urban Ministries, 169
Micah (biblical person), 107, 195–96
migrant, 8, 31, 149; *see also* immigrant
Migrant Protection Protocols, "Remain in Mexico," 31, 44
Mills, Michael, 99–100
minimum wage, 168–69
minority, 15, 32, 54, 57, 78, 95
Miranda, Tony, 20–22
mishpat, 5–6, 21, 22, 27–29
Mission Waco, Mission World, 133, 169–70
missionary, missions, 25, 35–36, 38, 62, 91, 103, 106, 122, 136, 148, 149, 198, 206–7
Mississippi, 90, 133, 135
Molinar, Bethany, 43–46
money, 2, 17, 47, 51, 63, 111, 145, 146, 147, 168–69, 172, 212; *see also* finances; income
money changers, 17, 47
Moorhead, Bea, 203–5
Mora, Nataly, 145–47
moral, morality, 5, 6, 23, 59–60, 62, 67, 78, 79, 131, 132, 144, 146, 158–59, 174, 177, 181, 201, 216; *see also* ethics, ethical
Moral Man and Immoral Society, 158
Morris County, Tex., 162
Morrison, Latasha, 190
Morrison, Toni, 130–32
mortality rate, 183, 208n2
mortgage, 64, 209–11; *see also* loan, lending
mother, 14, 15, 16, 31, 114, 124–26, 131, 145, 149, 154, 156, 161, 165, 177; *see also* parent, parents
Mother Teresa, 123
Mount Cristo Rey, 43
Müller, George, 69
Multiethnic Conversations: An Eight-Week Journey Toward Unity in Your Church, 153
murder, 28, 30, 40, 41, 104, 115, 117, 137, 143, 151–53, 161–63, 177, 179; *see also* killing
Muslim, 23–25, 109, 169
Mvskoke, Muscogee, Creek, 50–52
My Brother's Keeper, 169

228 — Index of Subjects

Nathan (biblical person), 197
National Immigration Forum, 153
nationalism, 107, 181
nationality, 62
Native, Native American, 28, 50–52, 95, 157
needy, 16, 122, 195, 210, 216
neglect, 59, 213
neighbor, neighborhood, 9, 13, 18, 21, 22, 24, 25, 44–45, 46, 64–66, 73, 81, 87, 109–12, 115, 116, 121, 127, 134, 135, 136, 145, 146, 147, 165, 169, 172, 180, 182–83, 194, 204–5, 211, 215
Nero (Roman Emperor), 185
New Deal, 124
New Testament, 3, 8–10, 21, 159, 175
Niebuhr, Reinhold, 100, 158
Nix, Christine Abel, 177–79
nonprofit, 44, 60, 76, 80, 116, 134, 156, 169, 206, 214
nonviolence, 121, 127, 137, 159, 164, 165
Northrup, Solomon, 131

Odessa, Tex., 124
Ogletree, John, 27–29
Oklahoma, 32, 50–51, 151
Okona, Nneka, 188
Okuwobi, Oneya Fennell, 153
Old Testament, 3, 5–7, 11, 27–28, 29, 38, 174, 196
One in Christ: Bridging Racial and Cultural Divides, 152, 153
Onesimus (biblical person), 184–87
opportunity, 2, 9, 31, 34, 53, 60, 75, 77, 78, 91, 94, 100, 101, 133, 140, 141, 158, 178–79, 181, 192, 198, 205, 209, 210, 211
oppress, oppressed, oppression, oppressor, 6, 7, 24, 31, 33, 45, 62–63, 80, 89, 102–3, 110–11, 122, 134, 157, 158, 159, 160, 175, 176, 180, 188, 189, 194–95, 201, 202, 216
organized crime, 30; *see also* gang, gangs
orphan, orphans, 69, 180, 210, 213
Orthodox, 9, 23, 25
Oxford Centre, Oxford, U.K., 38

Pacific Islander, 95
pain, 3, 63, 72, 75, 94, 104, 107, 108, 135, 146, 151, 152, 154, 167, 186, 189, 190, 206, 207–8
Palestine, Palestinian, 23–26
pandemic, 3, 33, 34, 59, 71, 86, 93, 96–97, 125, 162, 181n2, 188n1, 210, 216; *see also* COVID-19
parable, 18, 85, 92, 119–20, 146–47, 196
Paradise, 131
parent, parents, parenting, 14, 15, 30, 31, 41, 58–60, 86, 114, 127, 139, 140, 161–62, 174, 212
Park Cities Baptist Church, Dallas, 176
Parker, Rev. Joseph C., Jr., 61–63
partiality, 37, 61, 105, 118, 142, 144, 213, 214
pastor, pastors, preacher, priest, minister, 4, 9, 13, 14, 17, 18, 19, 20, 22, 27, 29, 31, 34, 36, 44, 54, 57, 63, 66, 70, 73, 79, 85, 88, 96, 100, 103, 108, 112, 115n2, 129, 135, 137, 138, 140, 145, 146, 147, 148–49, 150, 155, 164, 166, 170, 173, 176, 185, 187, 189, 196, 208
Pastors for Texas Children, 13
Patel, Hash, 161–62
Patel, Mitesh, 161
patients, 207–8
Paul (Apostle), 4, 37, 38, 68, 114, 184–86
payday loan, 28, 63, 75–76, 181
Paynter March, Suzii, 74–76
peace, peaceful, 4, 28, 33, 34, 35, 38, 68, 69, 96–98, 99, 114, 121, 142, 144, 151, 152, 155, 162, 164, 165
Perkins, John, 133
persecution, 24, 32, 128, 159
person/people of color, 52, 71, 121, 122, 136, 142, 143, 164, 189, 209
Pharaoh, 171–73
Pharisees, 47–48
Philadelphia, Pa., 91
Philemon (biblical person), 184–87
Pierce, Tim, 5–7
plead, 16, 134, 175, 180
Pledge of Allegiance, 28, 29, 183
Poitier, Sidney, 9
police, cops, 1, 28, 41, 42, 71, 83–85,

Index of Subjects — 229

104–5, 111, 113, 125, 132, 143, 155, 157, 164, 165, 173, 178, 188, 201, 205
police brutality, 28, 41, 42, 113, 125, 132, 157, 188
policy, policies, 12, 13, 29, 30, 31, 44, 45, 63, 83, 94, 110, 126, 165–66, 173, 178, 181, 183, 192, 193, 203–5, 209
political, politics, 2, 13, 21, 29, 65, 67, 69, 72, 95, 128, 143, 158n2, 159, 160, 173, 182, 183, 192, 193, 215
pollution, 182, 204
Polunsky Unit, Texas Department of Criminal Justice, 162
poor, poverty, 8, 16, 28, 29, 32, 58–60, 62, 64, 78, 91, 97, 111, 122, 124, 132, 134, 137, 157, 159, 167, 168–69, 172, 181n2, 182, 191, 192, 195, 207, 213, 216, 217
power, 2, 10, 13, 37, 39, 61–62, 63, 68, 75, 77, 94, 100, 107, 110, 111, 119, 121, 122, 131, 135, 146, 147, 155, 159, 160, 183, 185, 189, 195, 198, 213
pray, prayer, praying, 17, 19, 26, 27, 29, 30, 38, 44, 50, 68, 69, 87, 98, 118, 119–20, 126, 129, 130, 167, 176, 186, 210, 211
preach, preaching, sermon, 8, 9, 29, 62, 96, 97, 99, 114, 117, 130, 133, 135, 138, 148, 173, 185, 198, 217
pregnancy, 90, 183n12, 197, 206–8
prejudice, 37, 65, 72, 75, 129, 151, 173
premature birth, 126
pretrial, 168; *see also* trial
pride, 37
Primera Iglesia Bautista Dallas, 79
Primera Iglesia Bautista de Austin, 22
prison, prisoner, inmate, 8, 24, 33, 69, 84, 134, 136, 138, 155, 161–63, 166, 182n8, 184; *see also* felon, felony
prison guards, 84
private education, 13, 41
privilege, 9, 15, 32, 54, 59, 63, 74, 99, 109, 111, 125, 136, 149–50, 151, 155, 158, 176, 183, 190, 198, 210, 213
profiling, 28, 78
Project Still I Rise Inc., 116
property restrictions, 209
prophetic, prophets, prophecy, 4, 6, 7, 32, 64, 100, 107, 156, 160, 171, 172, 175, 183, 194, 195, 196, 210, 217

prosecutor, prosecution, 40, 104, 105, 165
Prosper Waco, 76, 156
prosperity, 194, 195, 210–11
prostitute, prostitution, 168
protect, protection, 6, 31–32, 33, 35, 41, 51, 69, 83, 84, 110, 114, 145, 147, 152, 157, 159, 165, 167, 183, 204, 212
protest, protester, 2, 63, 65, 71, 91, 113, 115, 121, 127, 132, 137, 143n4, 159, 164, 171, 211
Proverbs, 6, 16, 171, 172, 178, 180
Psalms, 6, 24, 27, 89, 119–20, 122, 142, 180, 197, 215
public education, 12–13, 14, 15–16, 28, 29, 124, 125
punish, punishment, 27–28, 40, 48, 68, 78, 154–56, 161–63
purpose, 1, 10, 13, 53, 55, 56, 57, 62, 77, 78, 151, 154, 177

race, racial, 2, 12, 20, 21, 25, 27, 28, 38, 39, 42, 52, 62, 63, 65, 66, 72, 73, 80–81, 86, 87, 91, 93, 102, 105, 109, 113, 117, 127, 128, 131, 132, 133, 135, 147, 152, 153, 154–55, 165, 182n6, 196, 201, 207, 208, 210
racial discrimination, 20, 125, 207
Racial Disparities in Incarceration Increase Acceptance of Punitive Policies, 165–66
racial disparity, 165–66, 192n8, 208n2
racial equality, inequality, 29, 33, 35, 39, 183n14, 207
racial injustice, 18, 20, 51, 65, 80–82, 104, 138, 168, 181–82, 200–202
racial justice, 80–82, 116, 153
racial reconciliation, 2, 20, 22, 81, 93, 94, 190n2
racism, 15, 19, 20, 37, 42, 45, 65, 72, 80–82, 86, 87, 93–94, 97, 107, 121, 122, 128, 132, 137, 166, 189, 200–202, 208
Rangel, Joe, 106–8
rape, 30–31, 40
read, reading, literacy, 1, 3, 4, 14, 30, 59, 113, 130–32, 135, 146, 148, 150, 167, 168, 189, 208, 210
reconciliation, reconcile, 2, 18, 20, 22, 45, 68, 81–82, 93, 94, 109, 110, 111, 122, 129, 138, 141, 190n2

230 — Index of Subjects

Reconstruction, 28
redemption, redeemed, 10, 33, 79, 93, 130, 135, 161–63, 176, 185, 198
redlining, 28, 64, 143
Reeves, Stephen, 180–83
reform, 32, 69, 123, 153, 165n1, 182n9
refuge, refugee, refugees, 30–32, 36, 44–45, 111, 131, 157, 181
Reid, Stephen, 8–10
Reina Valera (King James Bible, Spanish), 38
rejection, 23, 25, 79, 83, 93, 167, 181
relationship, 6, 11, 24, 81, 83–85, 94, 99, 110, 114, 115, 176, 182, 194, 201, 204, 217
religion, 12, 21, 32, 71, 105, 110, 111, 137, 158–59, 160, 171n1, 213
religious freedom, religious liberty, 32, 71
renew, renewal, 38, 69, 120, 152
repent, repentance, 18, 51, 94, 97, 134, 135, 145, 152, 198
rescue, 51, 122, 175
resettlement, 36
respect, 33, 35, 37, 39, 81, 91, 140, 142, 144, 150, 178, 208, 212, 213
responsibility, 21, 48, 52, 54, 60, 68, 118, 142–44, 149, 158, 178, 182, 189, 204, 210, 211, 217
resources, 12, 29, 34, 39, 44–45, 49, 83, 98, 111, 121, 145, 147, 153, 171, 172, 182
restoration, restore, 6, 18, 21, 62, 68, 75, 76, 105, 109, 110, 111, 161–63, 192, 197, 216
restitution, 180
Return to Justice, 51
Reyes, Albert, 37–39
Reyes, Gus, 139–41
rich, 181, 213; *see also* wealth, wealthy
right, rights, 2, 6, 12, 14, 16, 24, 27–29, 33, 34, 37, 40, 41, 45, 47, 48, 51, 53, 55, 57, 62, 63, 64, 66, 69, 79, 89, 90, 102–3, 105, 109, 110, 113, 115, 117, 122, 132, 133, 134, 140, 142, 143, 146, 151, 152, 159, 160, 164, 174–75, 176, 191, 194, 196, 200, 201–2, 210–11, 213, 216, 217
righteous anger, 17–19, 132
righteousness, *dikaiosuné*, 6, 7, 17, 18,

21, 22, 23, 27, 38, 53, 67, 68, 76, 89, 122, 131, 142, 143, 144, 146, 171, 173, 174, 175, 176, 180, 192, 194, 195, 197, 198, 215–17
Rincones, Jesse, 148–50
Rio Grande Valley, river, 59, 60, 78, 79
Robben Island, South Africa, 136–38
robbery, 17, 32, 146, 161, 180, 186
Robeson, Paul, 9
Rodriguez, Samuel, 175
Ross, Alyssa, 14–16

safety, security, 12, 15, 26, 30, 31, 32, 35, 59, 63, 65, 76, 93, 96–97, 105, 110, 111, 114, 119, 125, 127, 139, 156, 158, 163, 171, 173, 181n2, 192, 204, 210
salvation, 7, 9, 67, 68, 122, 126, 140, 161n2, 176, 197, 216, 217
Samaritan, 8–10, 65, 110, 111, 146–47
San Antonio, 55, 57, 66, 88, 161, 173, 193
sanctity of life, 111, 123
savings account, 59
SB4 (Texas, 2017), 109
scarcity, 171–73, 183
school, schools, 13, 14, 15, 16, 24, 29, 33, 41, 42, 54, 58, 59, 64–65, 71, 77, 79, 80, 82, 89, 90, 91, 92, 97, 99, 101, 107, 108, 110, 120, 124, 125–26, 127–28, 130, 150, 160, 169, 172, 173, 181–82, 183, 193, 217
school vouchers, 13
SCOTUSblog, 50
second chance, 75, 161–62
security: *see* safety
segregation, 24, 28, 62, 65, 128, 135, 142, 143, 155, 181–82, 209
self-actualization, 12
self-awareness, 12, 145, 146
Selma, Ala., 69
sensitivity training, 65, 88, 93, 189
sentencing, 42, 72, 105, 161–62, 165, 166, 182n8, 182n11
Sermon on the Mount, 117, 198
sex, sexuality, 65, 102, 105, 117, 208
sexual abuse, assault, exploitation, 34, 40, 91, 102, 103, 145, 190, 197
sexual perversion, 7
shalom, 109–12

Index of Subjects — 231

shaphat, 5–6
share, 39, 44, 48, 52, 66, 80, 94, 111,
    160, 163, 190, 202, 214
shelter, 30, 31, 44, 131, 169, 202
sibling, 33, 60, 114, 154, 212; *see also*
    brother; sister; family
sick leave, 172–73
silence, silent, 16, 18, 25, 63, 81, 97,
    114, 115, 120, 122, 123, 127, 128,
    130, 143, 144, 189
Silva, Diego, 58–60
Simmons, Chris, 19
Simon of Cyrene, 9–10
Simon the Cyrenian, 9
sin, sinner, 18, 28, 35, 37–38, 47, 48, 49,
    62, 65, 66, 67, 68, 74, 90, 94, 97, 107,
    126, 140–41, 151, 152, 174–75, 178,
    189, 197, 213
Singletary, Jon, 80–82
sister, 14, 18, 25, 33, 44–45, 52, 58, 66,
    73, 80, 88, 93, 96, 117, 135, 151–52,
    154, 213, 214; *see also* sibling; family
sit-in, 164
skin, skin color, 22, 23, 42, 69, 72, 73,
    86, 107, 127, 134, 140, 148–50, 182
slave, slavery, 28, 40, 69, 126, 128, 134,
    142, 171, 184–87, 200, 207
social capital, 126
social contract, 12
social justice, injustice, 7, 20, 21, 22, 59,
    94, 121, 122, 158, 175, 176, 217
social media, 2, 51, 64, 135, 177, 216
social work, 82, 92, 145, 147, 169, 193
socioeconomic, 59, 66, 72, 77, 78, 86,
    109
Soerens, Matthew, 153
solidarity, 21, 98, 100
Sorgwe, Felisi, 194–96
The Source, 206, 208
South Africa, 63, 136–38
southern (U.S.), 133, 200, 206
Spanish, 22, 38, 55–57, 146, 148–49, 176
speak, 1, 16, 17–19, 29, 48, 49, 50, 58,
    63, 87, 100, 115n2, 120, 121, 122,
    131, 142, 143–44, 159, 201
special education, 14
stability, 35, 77–79, 180
Stark College & Seminary, 85
status, 5, 27, 59–60, 77, 78, 81, 105,
    134, 145, 152, 165, 185, 208, 213

steal, 47, 87, 131, 162, 180
stereotype, stereotypes, 17, 65, 172
Stevenson, Bryan, 33, 113
stewardship, 158
stock market, 210
Stowers, Kirk, 83–85
stress, 59, 104, 125, 213
structure, structures, 37, 45, 59, 62, 80,
    81, 97, 142–43, 166, 204, 208
student, learner, 11, 20, 29, 54, 83, 95,
    105, 108, 109, 128, 145, 149, 167,
    182, 198, 207, 214
suffering, 20, 22, 28, 98, 102, 110, 135,
    149, 150, 161, 186, 188, 189, 190,
    208
Sugar Land Baptist Church, 103
suicide, 101, 193
Supplemental Nutrition Assistance
    Program, 192
Supplemental Security Income, 192
support, 11, 25, 51, 59, 65, 90, 91, 99,
    135, 161, 169, 178, 202, 204–5, 216
supremacy, 10, 28, 185, 188
Supreme Court, U.S., 50, 51, 117
suspect, 41, 177–79
suspicion, 12, 24, 42, 149
system, systems, 14, 20–21, 22, 28, 35,
    37, 41, 62–63, 71, 73, 77, 80–81, 84,
    97, 107, 115, 121–23, 136, 145, 152,
    154–55, 163, 165–66, 172, 178, 182,
    183, 187, 188, 191–93, 200–202, 207,
    209, 213
systemic racism, 72, 80–81, 107, 121,
    122, 136, 154–55, 165–66, 200–202,
    207, 209

Tatum, Beverly Daniel, 80
taxes, 12, 13, 60, 65
Taylor, Breonna, 1, 115, 123, 189
Taylor, Recy, 40
teacher, educator, professor, 4, 7, 8, 10,
    11, 14, 15, 16, 17, 30, 38, 42, 47, 48,
    51, 52, 54, 55, 57, 59, 68, 70, 74, 81,
    83, 92, 105, 108, 109, 114, 119, 120,
    125, 128, 132, 134, 144, 160, 176,
    179, 196, 197–99, 205, 209, 216, 217
teen, teenager: *see* youth
temple, Jerusalem, 17, 47
ten Boom, Corrie, 69
terror, 24, 31, 40

Texas, Texan, 1, 26, 73, 102–3, 104, 105, 106, 109, 126, 147, 148, 149, 161–63, 169, 179, 181n1, 183, 203, 205, 206, 207, 211

Texas Baptist Women in Ministry, 112

Texas Baptists, 3, 26, 29, 32, 49, 59n2, 73, 76, 123, 141, 156, 183; *see also* Baptist General Convention of Texas

Texas Christian Community Development Network, 46, 60, 170

Texas Coalition to Abolish the Death Penalty, 163

Texas Code of Criminal Procedure, 104

Texas Comptroller of Public Accounts, 203

Texas Impact, 205

theology, 25, 51, 52, 70, 120, 133, 145–46, 158–59, 196

therapy, therapist, 113, 189, 190, 191, 192, 200; *see also* counseling, counselor

Thinking Biblically About Immigrants & Immigration Reform, 153

Thirteenth Amendment, U.S. Constitution, 142

threat, 15, 33, 65, 99, 131, 144, 158, 177

Thurman, Howard, 159

Tisby, Jemar, 81

Title IX, 217

torture, 40, 207

transformation, 22, 37–38, 54, 57, 97, 98, 107, 129, 176, 185, 198

trauma, 45, 161, 163, 190, 192

Travis Baptist Church, Corpus Christi, 85

Treaty of 1866, 50

trial, 165, 168–69, 177

Trinity Baptist Church, San Antonio, 193

Truett Theological Seminary (Baylor), 10, 70, 92, 147

Truth, Sojourner, 69

truth, 12, 20, 26, 27, 51, 52, 63, 84, 97, 99, 100, 108, 117, 121, 123, 131, 133, 135, 153, 162, 166, 176, 189, 198, 199

tsedeq, tzedeq, 6, 21, 22

Tutu, Bishop Desmond, 63

undocumented, 109

Union Baptist Association, 29

United States, 10, 30, 31, 43, 44, 58, 77, 78, 96–97, 143, 151, 182, 207; *see also* America, American

unity, 4, 18, 25–26, 34, 35, 114, 115, 128–29, 135, 153, 166

Unity in the Community Coalition, 166

University of Mary Hardin-Baylor, 105

unnamed victims of crime, 177–79

Urban Institute, 96–97

Uriah the Hittite (biblical person), 197

U.S. House of Representatives, 117

USDA Center for Faith and Opportunity, 60

utilities, 58, 181

Uzziah (king of Judah), 195

values, 6, 21, 62, 83, 85, 94, 122–23, 130–31, 137, 145, 147, 152, 167–70, 207

Vanderpol, Gary, 51

vengeance, 67, 152

The Very Good Gospel: How Everything Wrong Can Be Made Right, 110

Vickrey, Garrett, 171–73

victim, victims, 29, 30, 32, 68, 89, 101, 102, 105, 117, 122, 154, 163, 177–79, 189, 217

violence, violent, 9, 32, 81, 130, 149, 161, 163, 173, 180, 188, 190, 195

Vivian, Rev. C.T., 132

voice, voiceless, 2, 73n1, 80, 88, 94, 99–100, 111, 158–60, 179, 189, 195, 213–14

vote, voting, 2, 28, 51, 109, 132, 164–65, 182, 216

voter suppression, restriction, 28, 182

Voting Rights Act, 28

vulnerable, vulnerability, 21, 34, 35, 44, 45, 58, 59, 67, 109, 110, 111, 131, 135, 145, 175, 181, 188, 189, 198

Waco, Tex., 76, 92, 133, 135, 156, 167–70, 187

Wake Forest Divinity School, 173

wall, border, 30, 43–46, 68, 169, 204

war, 24, 69, 93, 124, 132, 173, 209

Index of Subjects — 233

Wardlow, Billy Joe, 162–63
water, 17, 35, 73, 90, 99–100, 169, 180, 195
water fountain, 90
Waxman, Elaine, 96–97
Wayland Baptist University, 108, 197–99, 217
wealth, wealthy, 15, 77, 134, 181, 213; *see also* rich
weathering, 125–26
welcome, 25, 94, 107, 179, 201
Welcome the Stranger: Justice, Compassion, & Truth in the Immigration Debate, 153
welfare, 29, 51, 139, 217
welfare queen, 172
Wells, Ida B., 132
"We're in a New Age of Black Grief," 188
Werntz, Myles, 119–20
West Dallas Community School, 79
white, Anglo, 10, 15, 28, 29, 40, 41, 42, 51–52, 64–65, 80–81, 90, 93, 97, 102, 106, 109, 113, 115n2, 125–26, 128–29, 135, 136–38, 143, 154–55, 165–66, 167, 181–82, 188, 189, 190, 200, 201, 207, 208, 209
white flight, 65
White Fragility, 137
white supremacy, 10, 28, 188
Whitehurst, Rev. Mary, 206–8
"Who but the Lord?," 157
whole, wholeness, 4, 33, 34, 35, 75, 80, 109–11, 144, 216
widow, 119–20, 134, 175, 180, 213, 216
Wilberforce, William, 69
Willard, Dallas, 148, 150
Wilshire Baptist Church, Dallas, 211
Wilson, Patricia, 40–42
wisdom, wise, 6–7, 103, 118, 154, 156, 171–73, 191
witness, 17, 18, 54, 68, 71, 97, 109, 117, 131, 135, 137, 144, 145, 156, 179, 186, 188, 189
Wood, David, 84
Woodland Baptist Church, San Antonio, 173
woke, 74–75
woman, women, female, 1, 5, 8, 10, 14, 15, 17, 40, 47–48, 54, 56–57, 65, 75, 86, 87, 95, 100, 110–11, 112, 113, 124–26, 131, 134, 137, 151, 152, 157, 167, 169, 175, 190, 206–8
women's health, 206–8
work 2, 4, 9, 15, 26, 31, 32, 34, 35, 37, 38, 44, 46, 47, 52, 54, 57, 59, 62, 66, 68, 69, 74, 80, 81–82, 84, 87, 89, 91, 92, 93, 94, 96, 98, 99, 104, 105, 109, 111, 113, 115, 124, 129, 135, 137, 139, 140, 157, 167, 168–69, 172–73, 175, 176, 183, 185, 188, 190, 191–92, 193, 198, 203, 206, 209, 210, 211, 214; *see also* employment; job; labor
Works Progress Administration, 124
World Vision, 19
worth, 8, 34, 73, 100, 122–23, 131, 158, 163, 172, 205, 207
wrong, 2, 27, 28, 47, 68, 74, 85, 90, 95, 103, 107, 110, 113, 115, 121, 135, 138, 144, 151, 152, 175, 180, 191, 196, 212

xenophobia, 107

Yancey, Gaynor, 89–92
Yang, Jenny, 153
Young, Chris, 161–63
youth, adolescent, teenager, 15, 27–28, 34, 41, 58, 77, 78, 90, 101, 102, 112, 125, 148, 149, 161, 162, 164, 192, 216

Zacchaeus, 180
Zayasbazan, Jorge, 64–66
Zimmerman, George, 41

INDEX OF SCRIPTURE

Genesis

1:27	5, 121
2	11

Exodus

2:23–25	7
23:6	6

Leviticus

19	6
19:15	68, 213
19:17–18	9, 21, 180, 194
25	7

Numbers — 197

Deuteronomy

6:5	9, 194
10:17–19	68
16	6
16:20	21

Judges

17:6	79
21:25	79

1 Samuel

11	197

Esther

4:14	122

Job

29:7–25	216
35:14	6

Psalms

9:5	6
9:9	6
10	180
51:12–14	197
58:2	6
75:3	6
82:3	24
82:3–4	122
89:14	6, 27, 142, 215
97:2	122
103:6	89
140:13	6
149	180

Proverbs

1:3	6
2:9	6
8:6	6
10:12	178
18:1–2	172
21:3	6
29	180
31:5	6
31:8	6

Isaiah

1	180
1:17	24, 134, 175
3:14–15	195
5:23	195
6:8	179
33:15	6
42:1, 3–4	2
56:1–2	217
58:6–12	7

Index of Scripture — 235

Jeremiah

5:28	6, 210
21	180
22	180
22:16	6

Ezekiel

9:9	7

Daniel

11:6	6

Hosea

1–3	7

Amos

4:1	195
5	180
5:6–7	6
5:12	195
5:14–15	6, 29
5:24	6, 17, 195
8:5–6	195

Micah

2:1–2	195
3:1–2	195
6:8	6, 21, 27, 41, 53, 67, 94, 115, 139, 153, 160, 175, 196

Matthew

6:10	22, 153
6:33	21, 38, 198
7:12	123, 196
8	175
12:17–21	63, 156
16:24	10
19:19	180
20:32	63
21:12–13	17
22:34–40	8, 64, 116, 194, 216
25:31–46	8, 43, 45–46, 73, 122, 176, 180, 192
27:32	9
28:16–20	216

Mark

2	34
2:22	92
6:34–44	48
11:15–17	47
12:28–31, 33	8, 64, 180

Luke

4:18–19	134
10:25–37	8, 64, 146, 180
13:10–17	137
15:4–7	18
15:11–32	85
18:1–8	119–20, 196
19	180

John

3:16	153, 176
8:1–11	47, 175
13:35	144, 193

Acts

2:42–47	214
18:7	114

Romans

2:13	78
3:21–26	67
8:1–4	67
8:18–39	68
12:2	38
12:15	213
13:9	180

1 Corinthians

2:16	38
12:11, 18	54, 56
15:21	93

2 Corinthians

5:18	68
5:20	122

Galatians

3:28	68, 126, 134
5:14	180

Ephesians

2:15–16	68
4:2–6, 11–13	4
4:20–5:21	37

Colossians

1:20	68
2:15	62
4:9	185

2 Timothy

3:16–17	198

Philemon 184–87

Hebrews
11:1 69
12:2 8

2 Peter
3:13 68

James
1:27 213
2:8 180, 194

1 John
4:20–21 18

Revelation
7:9–12 153

CPSIA information can be obtained
at www.ICGtesting.com
Printed in the USA
LVHW101337190723
752345LV00001B/2